Evelyn Abbott

A Skeleton Outline of Greek History

Chronologically arranged

Evelyn Abbott

A Skeleton Outline of Greek History
Chronologically arranged

ISBN/EAN: 9783337311698

Printed in Europe, USA, Canada, Australia, Japan

Cover: Foto ©ninafisch / pixelio.de

More available books at **www.hansebooks.com**

A SKELETON OUTLINE

OF

GREEK HISTORY

CHRONOLOGICALLY ARRANGED

BY

EVELYN ABBOTT, M.A., LL.D.

FELLOW AND TUTOR OF BALLIOL COLLEGE, OXFORD

RIVINGTONS
WATERLOO PLACE, LONDON

MDCCCLXXXIV

PREFACE.

IN compiling these Outlines I have drawn from various sources. In the introductory portion, Ideler's *Handbuch der Chronologie* has been of the most service, though I owe something to J. Brandis's excellent monograph on early Greek chronology. The important work of A. Mommsen, *Chronologie*, etc., had not appeared when I wrote the section on the Calendar, but in regard to the Attic festivals I am indebted to the same writer's *Heortologie*. In the Tables I have used Fischer's *Zeittafeln*, which unfortunately only go down to 560 B.C.; Clinton's *Fasti Hellenici;* and the chronological table appended to the German edition of Curtius's *History of Greece*. In regard to the Peloponnesian war, Thucydides is, of course, sufficient; the period which follows is more confused, for no amount of ingenuity can introduce precision into the chronology of Xenophon. For the period of Demosthenes, A. Schaefer—*Demosthenes und seine Zeit*—is an admirable guide. Lastly, in regard to Alexander, I have used Dröysen and Grote.

For part of the Literary chronology, I have drawn largely on an admirable paper by Diels in the *Rheinisches Museum.*

The outlines of Athenian and Lacedaemonian Constitutional History are mainly taken from Schömann's *Antiquitates juris publici Graecorum.* The chronology of this part of Greek History is often so uncertain, that I did not venture to include it in the tables.

E. Λ.

ERRATA.

B.   A.

Page 37, *place* 5 Mermnadae. *under* 22 Heracleids=505 years.
Page 59, *for* 765 B.C., OL. 2.3, *read* 770 B.C., OL. 2.3.
Page 63, *for* 673 B.C., OL. 27.1, *read* 672 B.C., OL. 27.1.
Page 71, anno 515, *read* Miltiades *for* Miltiades III.
Page 78, anno 459, *omit.*
Page 81, anno 436, *omit* Cratinus the comic poet.
Page 84, anno 429, *add* Death of Pericles.
Page 118, *add* the Olympiads 101.4 *under* 373, *and* 102.1 *under* 372.

CONTENTS.

Part I.

CHRONOLOGY AND GENEALOGIES.

CHRONOLOGY—
		PAGE
I.	Sources of our knowledge of Greek Chronology, and the difficulties attending it,	7
II.	The Greek Calendar,	10
	a. Definitions, Cycles,	10
	b. Names of the Attic months,	14
	c. Prytanies,	15
	d. Division of the month,	15
III.	Attic Festivals,	16
IV.	Rules for reducing Olympiads into Years B.C. and *vice versa*,	18

GENEALOGIES—
I.	Argive (Earlier),	21
II.	Argive (Later),	22
III.	The Pelopids,	23
IV.	Kings of Lacedaemon,	24
	Note on the List of Spartan Kings,	25
V.	Argive Kings from the Return to Pheidon,	26
VI.	List of Messenian Kings,	27
VII.	List of Kings of Corinth,	28
VIII.	Kings of Attica,	29
	Note on the Attic List,	30

		PAGE
IX.	Cretan Kings,	31
X.	Aeacids,	32
XI.	Kings of Thebes,	33
XII.	The Hellenes,	34
XIII.A.	Kings of Macedonia,	35
XIII.B.	Details of the later Kings,	36
XIV.	Second Assyrian Empire,	37
XV.	Kings of Egypt,	38
XVI.	Lydian Kings,	39
XVII.	Kings of Media,	40
XVIII.	Second Babylonian Empire,	41
XIX.	Athenian Families,	42
XX.	Athenian Archons,	43
XXI.	List of Victors in the Stadium or Foot-race at Olympia,	47

Part II.

CHRONOLOGICAL TABLES.

I. From the Trojan War to the First Olympiad,	55
Note on the Date of the Trojan War,	57
Note on the Date of Lycurgus,	59
II. The Olympiads,	61

Part III.

Constitutional History of Athens and Lacedaemon,	147

PART I.

CHRONOLOGY AND GENEALOGIES

CHRONOLOGY.

I.

Sources of our knowledge of Greek Chronology, and the difficulties attending it.

In all ancient chronology we must distinguish the dates which have come down to us on the authority of ancient writers from those which we attempt to fix ourselves by various computations. In regard to the first, we have to inquire what is the value of the authority from which we have received the date, and what means had our authority of fixing it. For even if we allow that records of events were kept for a long time before any attempt was made at a systematic chronology, these records were nevertheless arranged according to the magistrates or kings of the cities in which the events occurred; there was no general era in existence, by which the various records could be brought into accurate relation to each other.

The list of the *priestesses of Argos* (the oldest list used in chronology) was published by Hellanicus, the elder contemporary of Herodotus, who also published a list of the victors in the Carnean Festival at Sparta. The same author seems to have revised the early *Attic chronology*. He may have had access to archives of the Neleid families, but in some points it is clear that his computations are mere fictions, invented with the object of bringing the chronology into a certain fixed scheme, and Thucydides thought it necessary to speak of the want of accuracy in the chronology of Hellanicus for the period between the Persian and Peloponnesian wars. Lists of the *Spartan kings* were in existence in the time of Herodotus. The list of the *Olympic victors* was published by Hippias of Elis, but it was not made the basis of chronology till Timaeus of Tauromenium (B.C. 264).

Other lists were those of the *archons at Athens*, first published by Demetrius of Phalerum, and of the *ephors of Sparta*.

The first scholar who attempted to draw up a systematic chronology was Eratosthenes of Alexandria (B.C. 240), whose labours were the foundation of all that came after. His work was epitomised and corrected by Apollodorus (B.C. 140). This smaller work, which was composed in verse, became the standard manual on the subject in antiquity. If we possessed the works of these great chronologists entire, we should be in a much better position than we are, for the later writers (Eusebius, Jerome, Syncellus, Africanus), from whom our dates have come to us, copied and misunderstood them. Even in Eusebius we find that one and the same man and event is attributed to different years, a confusion which must have arisen from combining more than one work on chronology in his own treatise. In Suidas things are even worse; we have mere blunders, a man's *floruit* being put for his birth, or *vice versa*. As a rule, the later the authority the worse it is, because there is less of intelligent work, and more of slavish copying.

But even the best works on chronology in antiquity seem to have laboured under certain deficiencies, which were perhaps unavoidable at the time. *Reigns* are not distinguished from *generations*. The average length of a generation may be put at 30 or $33\frac{1}{3}$ years (three generations making up a century), but reigns are shorter, and an average of 25 years is perhaps as much as can be allowed. On this calculation, nine generations make 300 years, but nine reigns make only 225 years. But it will be seen from the lists of early kings in Corinth, Sparta, and Argos (given below), that even $33\frac{1}{3}$ years are below the average of the reigns which are required to cover the time between the first Olympiad and the traditional dates of such events as the Trojan War and the Return of the Heracleids.

Again, attempts were made to *reduce the chronology to system*. In the scheme of Attic chronology attributed to Hellanicus, the same number of years is assumed for the reign of the Neleid family at Athens, and for the interval between

Cecrops and the Fall of Troy, and in order to bring this about, the old Attic kings are increased from four to nine. Again, striking events are made to *synchronise,* so that even in the time of Herodotus the battles of Himera and Salamis are supposed to have occurred on the same day. Or great men are brought into connection with each other, and we get a date for the Seven Wise Men. Or the precise date of a man's birth was unknown, and his period had to be fixed by his connection with some well-known public event. Lastly, it was common in Greek history to attribute a number of events, differing by many years, to one and the same person. The date attributed to Lycurgus may have varied with the reforms attributed to him.

With regard to received dates then, a student of chronology has first to ascertain, whenever he can, whether the date which he finds in Eusebius and Syncellus is derived from Eratosthenes or some other good authority, and then to inquire what grounds Eratosthenes had for fixing it.

A distinction is generally drawn between the chronology of the events up to the date of the first Olympiad (776 B.C.), and of the events beyond it. The first are regarded as fixed and certain, the second as legendary. Eusebius, *Praep. Evang.* x. 10, μέχρι μὲν 'Ολυμπιάδων οὐδὲν ἀκριβὲς ἱστόρηται τοῖς Ἕλλησι, πάντων συγκεχυμένων καὶ κατὰ μηδὲν αὐτοῖς τῶν πρὸ τοῦ συμφωνούντων. ("Down to the Olympiads nothing accurate has been recorded by the Greeks, everything being in confusion and full of discrepancies.") It is, in fact, pretty certain that the Greeks had, or believed that they had, an accurate record of years from the first Olympiad, by which events could be dated, and that before the first Olympiad they fixed dates by genealogies. As the genealogies differed, the dates fixed upon them differed. Hence there were many different dates for the capture of Troy.

Whenever we have a reference, in connection with a historical event, to an eclipse or any other astronomical phenomenon, we are of course, enabled to fix the date with accuracy. There is, for instance, no doubt about the beginning of the Peloponnesian War, or of the retreat from Syracuse. Some check of this kind is absolutely necessary in the great confusion of ancient calendars, owing to which all attempts to fix the *day* of events, at any rate before the invention of the Metonic Cycle at Athens in 432 B.C., are extremely doubtful.

Other dates can of course be fixed approximately by their relation to events of which the date is known. Thus the chronology of the Lydian and Persian monarchs depends on the date of the capture of Sardes by Cyrus, and it will vary by a few years according to the date established for that event. Many of the events recorded by Herodotus can only be fixed vaguely, as they come after or before other events; and, in fact, whatever the historical value of the list of Olympic victors may be, there are comparatively few dates in Greek history before 432 B.C. which can be fixed with precision.

II.

THE ATTIC CALENDAR.

a. Definitions, Cycles.

A day is a revolution of the sun. This may be calculated from one culmination to another, *i.e.* from the time when the sun touches the meridian to the time when he touches it again, and the meridian may be the day meridian (mid-day) or the night meridian (midnight), which is the point from which we calculate our day. Or it may be calculated from sunrise to sunrise, or from sunset to sunset, but in this case the length of the day, unless corrected, will vary greatly.

Hours, minutes, and seconds are divisions of the day.

A month is the period

  (1), in which the moon performs her orbit. This is *a periodic month*, 27 days, 7 hrs., 43′, 5″ in length;
  (2), which elapses between one conjunction of the sun and moon and another, *a Synodic month*. The sun advances while the moon is performing her orbit, and the space over which he has advanced must be

THE ATTIC CALENDAR.

made up before she can again overtake him. This is the month used in calendars; the average length is 29 days, 12 hrs., 44', 3".

A year is the period in which the year returns
(1), to the same star, *a sidereal year*, 365 days, 6 hrs., 9', 10";
(2), to the same place in the equator, *a tropical year*. This is somewhat shorter than the sidereal year, owing to the precession of the equinoxes; it is roughly 365¼ days in length. This is the year used in calendars.

Our calendar is arranged on the solar year, the moon being disregarded. This basis of computation was derived from Egypt, where from a very early time a solar year was known, consisting of twelve months of 30 days, with five days added. The Egyptians were also aware that this year was too short by a quarter of a day. But it was late before the Greeks became acquainted with this computation. For a long time they reckoned by lunar months, and were indeed ignorant of the exact length of these. They assumed it to be 29½ days, and as they allowed twelve months to the year, they thus obtained a year of (29½ × 12 =) 354 days. They did not divide the months equally; six were "full" months of 30 days, and six were "hollow" months of 29 days, the full and the hollow months alternating regularly. It was soon discovered that such a year was too short; and the defect was remedied by inserting intercalary months (ἐμβολιμαῖοι). Of the mode in which the insertion was made in the earliest times, we have no knowledge; the additional months could not be inserted with any degree of accuracy till cycles had been arranged in which the moon and the seasons of the year were supposed to coincide, *i.e.* in which the months which depended on the moon and the years which were governed by the sun were commensurable. The discrepancy between the two would be noticeable in ancient Greece, even though they had no solar year, because the festivals were fixed (like our Easter) by the moon, and many operations of husbandry were fixed by the rising of constellations, etc. The relative position of the two would be found to change as the lunar years fell behind the true time.

It may have been Solon to whom the Athenians owed the regular arrangement of full and hollow months in the year (IDELER, i. 266). He also named the last day of the month ἔνη καὶ νέα as belonging to both months, the old and the new, and gave the name νουμηνία to the day on which the moon was first visible, *i.e.* to the day *after* the conjunction from which the month really dates.

A month calculated at $29\frac{1}{2}$ days is 44' 3" short of the full length, hence a year of 12 such months is about 9 hours too short for the lunar time. It is also $11\frac{1}{4}$ days behind the solar year. The first attempt at correction was to insert every other year an intercalary month of 30 days. This gave $354 + 354 + 30 = 738$ days for 25 months; *i.e.* each month averaged $29\frac{13}{25}$ days, which was nearly correct. But two solar years amount to $730\frac{1}{2}$ days, so that the double year of 25 lunar months was in excess of two solar years by $7\frac{1}{2}$ days.

This was perhaps the system of Solon. It could have been made tolerably correct by leaving out a month of 30 days in every eight years, *i.e.* by intercalating three, not four, months in the eight years. This consideration may have led the Greeks to their octennial cycle, of which Geminus gives the following account (IDELER, i. 294).

"Discovering the imperfection of their *trieteric* system (such is the Greek form for a system extending to two years, διὰ τρίτου ἔτους), the Greeks established an octennial cycle, containing 2922 days in 99 months, three being intercalary. The lunar year contains 354 days, the solar year $365\frac{1}{4}$; the latter therefore has $11\frac{1}{4}$ days in excess of the former. Now $11\frac{1}{4}$ days, if multiplied by eight, gives 90 days, or three months of 30 days; thence in eight years the lunar time is three months (90 days) behind the solar. This led to the insertion of three months in a cycle of eight years. These intercalary months were inserted at even intervals as far as possible, in the third fifth, and eighth year." But, as Geminus proceeds to point out, the length assumed for the lunar month ($29\frac{1}{2}$ days) was incorrect. He puts it at $29\frac{1}{2}$ days + $\frac{1}{33}$ of a day. Ninety-nine months on this computation would make up $2923\frac{1}{2}$ days, but eight solar years make up 2922 days ; *i.e.* in a cycle of eight years, the lunar time is a day and a half in excess of the solar time. The discrepancy can be remedied by adding three days to the solar time in sixteen years, but this remedy makes the solar time three days too long in sixteen years, or 30 days too long in 160 years. The system was therefore corrected by leaving out one intercalary month in 160 years.

Even this is incorrect. The lunar month, even as fixed at $29\frac{1}{2}$ and $\frac{1}{33}$ days was found to be 25" too short (according to the calculation of Hipparchus). In 160 years, 25" a month amounts to a deficiency of 13 hours, and as the month of 30 days, omitted once in 160 years, is 11 hours too long for a lunar month, the deficiency (11+13 hours) was made up by adding one day in 160 years.

Whether these corrections were ever carried out is doubtful ; they were probably superseded by a better system, before sufficient time had elapsed to put into practice the corrections which had been made in theory. In 432 B.C., Meton invented a different cycle, consisting of 19 years. In 19 years there are 6940 days and 235 months, including 7 intercalated months, and each year averages $365\frac{5}{19}$ days. The 235 months were divided into 110 full and 125 hollow. The regular alternation of full and hollow was discontinued, every 64th day being omitted, in order to bring down 7050 days (235 months ×30 days) to the required number of 6940.

This period was faulty in regard to the solar year, which was $\frac{1}{76}$ of a day too long. It was therefore corrected by Calippus, who instituted a cycle of 76 years = four Metonic cycles, and omitted a day in each cycle. This period was regarded by Geminus as the most accurate.

The cycle of Meton was invented in Ol. 87.1. = 432 B.C., but whether it was at once adopted or not is doubtful. Boeckh thinks that it was not, and that for some time at any rate, the Athenians went on with the octennial cycle as corrected by the solar year of $365\frac{1}{4}$ days, which Eudoxus, the friend of Plato, borrowed from Egypt. But whenever introduced, the cycle dates from July 16, 432 B.C. This was the first day of Hecatombaeon, in the first year of the first cycle of nineteen years.

b. *Names of the Attic months.*

The following are the names of the Attic months. The exact day on which the year began varied; but, speaking roughly, the Attic months corresponded to the English months opposite :—

Hecatombaeon,	July.
Metageitnion,	August.
Boedromion,	September.
Pyanepsion,	October.
Maemacterion,	November.
Poseideon,	December.
Gamelion,	January.
Anthesterion,	February.
Elaphebolion,	March.
Munychion,	April.
Thargelion,	May.
Scirophorion,	June.

When an intercalary month was needed it was placed after Poseideon, as Poseideon II.

The Attic year thus began at the summer solstice, and in this respect coincided with the Olympic year. Whether this was always the case is doubtful; from the position of the intercalary month, which would naturally come at the end of the year, it seems not improbable that the year once began at the winter solstice, as with us.

c. *Prytanies.*

The *civic* year of the Athenians was not reckoned by months, but by prytanies. The ten tribes of Cleisthenes were represented by fifty prytanies for each, and these held office in an order established by lot at the beginning of the year. The time during which each tribe held office was a "prytany;" the tribe in office was the presiding tribe. In an ordinary year of 354 days, the first six prytanies consisted of 35 days each, the last four of 36 (IDELER, i. 289), but in an intercalary year the prytanies would rise to 38 and 39 days.

d. *Division of the month.*

The Attic month was divided into three decades. The first day of the month was the νουμηνία, and as a rule began with the first appearance of the moon in the evening, for the Attic day began at sunset. The actual conjunction of sun and moon was νουμηνία κατὰ σελήνην (THUC. ii. 28).

The first ten days of the month were reckoned in the order of the numbers, the word ἱσταμένου being added, *e.g.*

1. νουμηνία.
2. δευτέρα ἱσταμένου.
3. τρίτη ἱσταμένου.
4. τετάρτη ἱσταμένου.
5. πέμπτη ἱσταμένου.
6. ἕκτη ἱσταμένου.
7. ἑβδόμη ἱσταμένου.
8. ὀγδόη ἱσταμένου.
9. ἐννάτη ἱσταμένου.
10. δεκάς or δεκάτη ἱσταμένου.

The days from the tenth to the twentieth were reckoned by their number with the addition ἐπὶ δέκα.

11. πρώτη ἐπὶ δέκα.
12. δευτέρα ἐπὶ δέκα, etc.
20. εἰκάς.

The days from the twentieth to the last day of the month

were known as the εἰκάδες. From the twenty-first, they were calculated, like Roman time, backwards from the end of the month, and the word φθίνοντος was added; *e.g.* in a full month;
    21. δεκάτη φθίνοντος.
    22. ἐννάτη φθίνοντος.
    23. ὀγδόη φθίνοντος.
    24. ἑβδόμη φθίνοντος.
    25. ἕκτη φθίνοντος.
    26. πέμπτη φθίνοντος.
    27. τετάρτη or τετρὰς φθίνοντος.
    28. τρίτη φθινόντος.
    29. δευτέρα φθίνοντος.
    30. ἕνη καὶ νέα.
In a "hollow" month, with 29 days, the twenty-first day would be ἐννάτη φθίνοντος.

III.
ATTIC FESTIVALS.

Hecatombaeon.
XII.	Cronia.
XVI.	Synœcia.
XXIV.-XXIX.	Great Panathenaea.
XXVII.-XXVIII.	Little Panathenaea.

Metageitnion has no festivals.

Boedromion.
III.	Niceteria.
V.	Genesia.
VI.	Marathon festival.
XIII.	Proerosia.
XVI.-XXV.	Eleusinia.

Pyanepsion.
VI.	Kybernesia.
VII.	Pyanepsia and Oscophoria.

VIII.-IX.	Thesea.
X.	Stenia.
XI.	Thesmophoria.
XII.-XIV.	Thesmophoria in the city.
XXVII.-XXIX.	Apaturia.
XXX.	Chalcea.

Maemacterion.

XIX.-XXI.	Zeus Georgos.

Poseideon.

VIII.-XI.	Piraea.

Gamelion.

VIII.-XI.	Lenaea.
XXVII.	Gamelia.

Anthesterion.

XI.-XIII.	Anthesteria.
XIX.-XXI.	Little Mysteries.
XXIII.	Diasia.

Elaphebolion.

VIII.-XIII.	Great Dionysia.
XIV.	Pandia.

Munychion.

VI.	Delphinia.
XVI.	Munychia.
XIX.	Olympia.

Thargelion.

VI.-VII.	Thargelia.
XIX.	Callynteria.
XX.	Bendidea.
XXV.	Plynteria.

Scirophorion.

XII.	Scirophoria.
XIII.	Arrephoria.
XIV.	Buphoria.

IV.

Rules for reducing Olympiads into Years b.c.
and vice versa.

(1.) Remember that Ol. 1. 1. means the year extending from July 776 B.C. to July 775 B.C., and that each Olympiad is equal to four years.

Hence, in order to reduce Olympiads to years B.C., the number of Olympiads must be multiplied by four, and the odd years (if any) must be added in. Thus: Ol. 70. 3. must become $70 \times 4 + 3 = 283$.

But we cannot at once deduct 283 from 776, because Ol. 1. 1. (which is included in the multiplication by four) gives $1 \times 4 + 1 = 5$ for the first Olympiad—which is our starting-point.

Add therefore 5 to 776 B.C. before subtracting the Olympiads multiplied as above, *e.g.*
$$781 - 283 = 498 \text{ for Ol. 70. 3.}$$

(2.) Conversely, when reducing years B.C. to Olympiads, add 5 to 776, then deduct the years B.C. and divide the result by four, *e.g.* to find the Olympiad for 500 B.C.

$$776 + 5 = 781$$
$$500$$
$$\overline{281}$$

$\dfrac{281}{4} = 70.$ 1. the Olympiad corresponding to 500 B.C.

(3.) In each case this process will give the year in which the Olympic year begins, *i.e.* Ol. 70. 3. began July 498, ended July 497.

GENEALOGIES.

I.

ARGIVE GENEALOGIES

(Earlier).

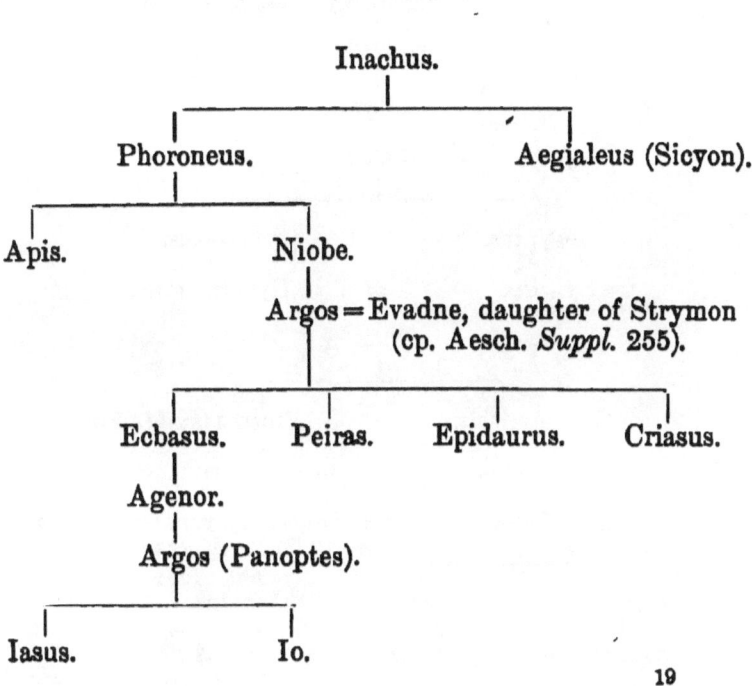

II.
ARGIVE GENEALOGIES
(Later).

Inachus. (Grote, pt. i. c. 4.)
|
Io *(wanders to Egypt)*.
|
Epaphus.
|
Libya.
|
Belus.
|
┌─────────────┴─────────────┐
Aegyptus.   Danaus.
| |
Lynceus.   =   Hypermnestra.
            |
          Abas.
            |
   ┌────────┴────────┐
Acrisius.   Proetus *(builds Tiryns)*.
   | |
Danae.   Megapenthes.
   |
Perseus.   *(Perseus and Megapenthes exchange,*
           Perseus builds Mycenae.)
   |
┌──────────┬──────────────┐
Electryon.   Alcaeus.   Sthenelus.
   | | |
Alcmene = Amphitryon.   Eurystheus *(slain with his sons in Attica, cousin to Agamemnon).*
            |
         Heracles.
(Date of Troy.) |
         Hyllus.
            |
         Cleodaeus.
            |
         Aristomachus.
            |
   ┌────────┼──────────────┐
Temenus. Aristodemus.   Cresphontes.
(Argos.) *(Sparta.)*   *(Messenia.)*
   | |
Eurystheus.   Procles.
(p. 22.)   (p. 22.)

III.

The Pelopids. (Grote, i. 7.)

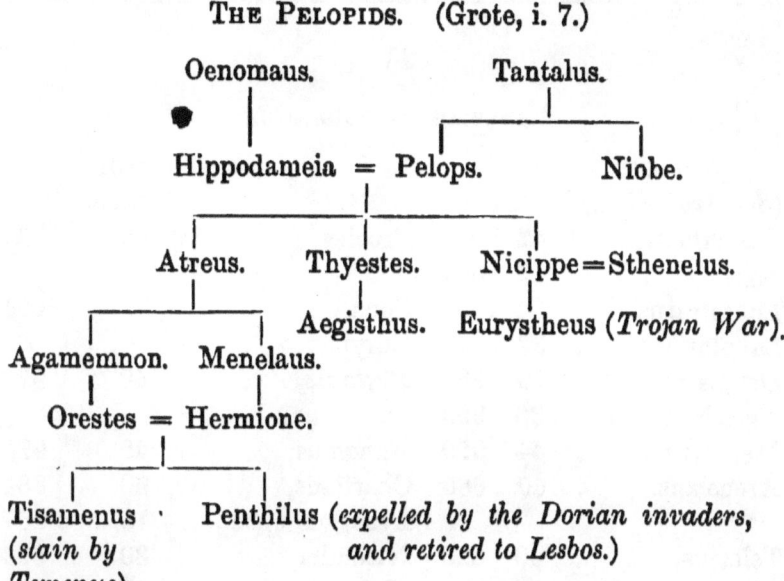

The rightful heirs to the throne of Argos were Heracles and his sons, who were exiles at Thebes, whither Amphitryon the father of Heracles had retired, after slaying his uncle Electryon. But they were set aside and kept from their right by Eurystheus. Hence the "Return" of the Heracleids was the recovery of an inheritance.

The difficulty of bringing Atreus and the Pelopids to Argos (they belong to Pisa) was deeply felt by ancient authorities (see Thuc. i. 9). In Homer, Pelops is known as πλήξιππος (Il. ii. 104), and gives to Atreus the sceptre which he has received from Hermes. The peninsula is first called "the island of Pelops" in Tyrtaeus.

IV.

KINGS OF LACEDAEMON.

AGIADS. (*See Argive list.*)	YRS.	B.C.	EURYPONTIDS.	YEARS.	B.C.
Eurystheus,	42	1103	Procles,	49	1103
Agis,	2	1061			
Echestratus,	34	1059	Sous,		1054
Labotas,	37	1025	Eurypon,		?
Doryssus,	29	988	Prytanis,	49	978
Agesilaus,	30	959			
Menelaus,	44	929	Eunomus,	45	929
Archelaus,	60	885	Charilaus,	60	884
			Lycurgus πρόδ.,	18	884-867
Teleclus,	40	825	Nicander,	39	824
Alcamenes,	27	785	Theopompus,	47	785

[The first Olympiad 776 falls in the tenth year of Alcamenes and Theopompus, according to Apollodorus, but if Theopompus lived to the end of the first Messenian war (724 B.C.), this is hardly possible (Tyrtaeus, *Frag.* 5. Bergk).]

Polydorus,	$7\frac{58}{53}$		Anaxandrides.	
Eurycrates,			Zeuxidamus, 738	Archidamus.
Anaxander,			Anaxidamus,	Anaxilaus.
Eurycratidas,			Archidamus I.,	Leotychides I., c. 635.
Leon,			Agasicles,	Hippocratides.
Anaxandrides,	c. 560		Ariston, c. 560.	
Cleomenes,	c. 520-488		Demaratus (*banished*), c. 510-491	
Leonidas,	488-480		Leotychides,	22 491-469
Pleistarchus,	480-458			
{ Cleombrotus πρόδικος, 480				
{ Pausanias πρόδ. 480-c. 468				
Pleistoanax *banished*,	50	458-445	Archidamus II.,	42 469-427

AGIADS.			EURYPONTIDS.		
Nicomedes	YRS.	B.C.		YRS.	B.C.
πρόδ.,	.	458- ?			
Pausanias,	.	445-426			
Cleomenes πρόδ.,		445- ?			
Pleistoanax *again*,		426-408	Agis I.,	29	427-398
Pausanias *again*, banished,	. 14	408-394			
Agesipolis,	. 14	394-380	Agesilaus,	41	397-361
Aristodemus πρόδ.,		394- ?			
Cleombrotus,	. 9	380-371			
Agesipolis II.,	1	371-370	Archidamus III.,	23	361-338
Cleomenes II.,	61	370-309	Agis II.,	9	338-331
			Eudamidas I.,		330-[305]
Areus I.,	. 44	309-265			
Acrotatus,	.	265	Archidamus IV.,		[305-209]
Areus II.,	. 8	264-256			
Leonidas πρόδ.,		264-256			
Leonidas II. *(banished)*,		256-243			
Cleombrotus (do.),		243-240	Agis III.,	4	244-240
Leonidas II. again,		240-236	Eurydamidas,		239-236
Cleomenes III. (221),		236-223	(Archidamus V., *Pretender*).		
Eucleidas,	.	236-223			
Agesipolis,	.	221			
Lycurgus,	.	221-210	Machondas,		210-207
(Pelops,	.	210-207)	Nabis,	.	207-192

NOTE ON THE LIST OF SPARTAN KINGS.

If we deduct ten years for Alcamenes and Theopompus—the first Olympiad falling in the tenth year of each—we get 317 years from the beginning of Alcamenes and Theopompus to the Trojan war $(10 + 317 + 776 = 1103)$. In this period we have nine names of Agiad kings (including Menelaus, who is omitted in most lists) and eight names of Eurypontids. This allows an average of 35 and 39 years for a reign, which is from 10 to 14 years too high. (*See Note on date of Trojan war*, p. 55.)

V.

ARGIVE KINGS FROM THE RETURN TO PHEIDON.

Temenus (*See Argive list*, p. 20).
Ceisus.
Medon.
Thestius.
Merops.
Aristodamidas.
Pheidon.

The date of Pheidon is 748 B.C., in which year he celebrated the eighth Olympic festival. Here, therefore, we have but seven names for the 355 years between 748 and 1103, *i.e.* an average of 50 years for a reign, or more than double the common length.

VI.

LIST OF MESSENIAN KINGS.

Cresphontes (*see Argive list*, p. 20).
Aepytus.
Glaucus.
Isthmius.
Dotadas.
Sybotas.
Phyntas.
Antiochus (*Messenia becomes a part of Sparta*).

This brings us from the Return down to 743, the beginning of the first Messenian war (acc. to Pausanias); here, therefore, we have eight names for 360 years, which gives an average of 45 years to each.

VII.

List of Kings of Corinth.

These, like the Spartan and Argive and Messenian kings, claim to be descendants of Heracles (Duncker, *Hist. Greece*, bk. iii. c. 3).

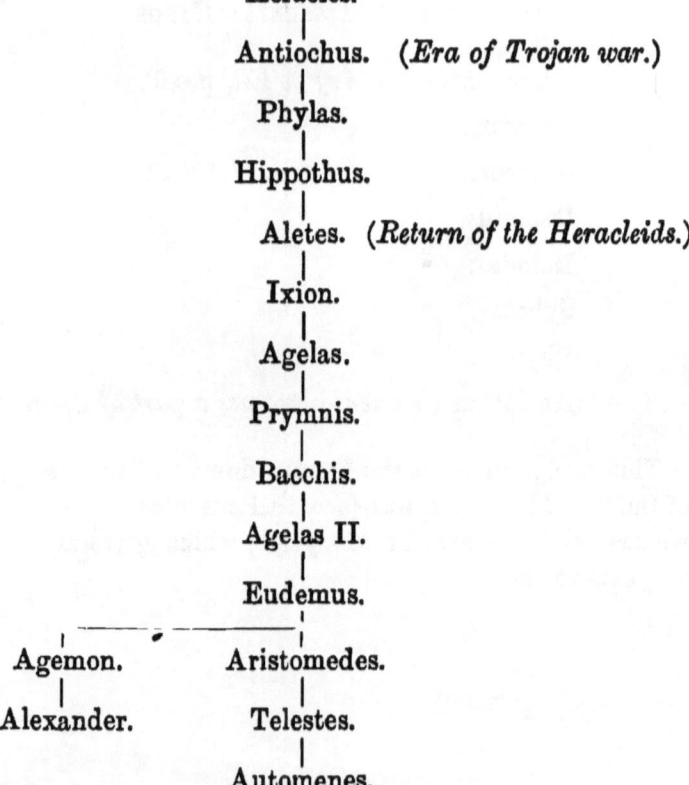

Heracles.
|
Antiochus.   (*Era of Trojan war.*)
|
Phylas.
|
Hippothus.
|
Aletes.   (*Return of the Heracleids.*)
|
Ixion.
|
Agelas.
|
Prymnis.
|
Bacchis.
|
Agelas II.
|
Eudemus.
|
Agemon.   Aristomedes.
| |
Alexander.   Telestes.
      |
      Automenes.

Telestes was slain 747 B.C.; Automenes reigned but one year, when annual prytanies were established of the family of the Bacchiadae. Thus from Aletes to Telestes inclusive, we have nine generations (including Agelas II.) and eleven reigns (including Agemon and Alexander, who were collateral), to bring us from 747 to 1103, the date of the Return. This gives more than 39 years for a generation and more than 32 years for a reign, both of which numbers are above the average.

VIII.
Kings of Attica.
A.—Erechtheidae.

Cecrops,	50 (years).	1606 B.C.
Cranaus,	10.	
Amphictyon,	40.	
Erichthonius,	10.	
Pandion I.,	50.	
Erechtheus,	40.	
Cecrops II.,	53.	
Pandion II.,	43.	
Aegeus,	48.	
Theseus,	31.	
Menestheus,	23.	(*Fall of Troy.*) 1209 B.C.

B.—Theseidae.

Demophon, 36 years.

Oxyntas, 14 „

Apheidas, 1.   Thymaetas, 9.

C.—Neleidae.

Melanthus, 37 years.   1149 B.C.

Codrus, 21 „

D.—Medontidae.

Medon,	20 (years).	(*The "Kings" were now called "Archons."*)
Acastus,	39.	
Archippus,	40.	
Thersippus,	14.	
Phorbas,	43.	
Megacles,	28.	
Diognetus,	28.	
Theracles,	15.	
Ariphron,	30.	
Thespieus,	40.	
Agamestor,	26.	
Aeschylus,	23.	(*The second year of Aeschylus* =776 B.C.
Alcæmon,	2.	

In the second year of Alcmaeon (= 752 B.C.), the life archons came to an end, and archons for ten years were established. Of these there were seven :—

Charops,	752 B.C.	Leocrates,	712 B.C.
Aesimedes,	742 ,,	Apsander,	702 ,,
Clidicus,	732 ,,	Eryxias,	692 ,,
Hippomenes,	722 ,,		

NOTE ON THE ATTIC LIST.

This list was perhaps compiled by Hellanicus, who in constructing it may have followed the dates preserved in the archives of Pisistratus and his sons, the lineal descendants of the Neleid kings. The total number of years from 752 B.C., when the Neleid family ceased to have the exclusive possession of the archonship, up to Melanthus, with whom the family begins, is 397 years, and the average allowed for the reigns and archons is not to be regarded as excessive, because we have nothing to prove that the archonship passed from father to son. But this interval of 397 years is repeated for the time which elapsed between the TROJAN WAR and CECROPS. In this period the old Attic tradition presented only six names, Cecrops, Erechtheus, Pandion, Aegeus, Theseus, and Menestheus; and when these six have been raised to eleven, as in the list given, we have an average of 36 years for a reign, which is about 13 years more than we can allow.

The computation of Eratosthenes was different; he placed Cecrops in 1556 B.C., the Fall of Troy in 1183, the date of Melanthus in 1127. Moreover, while the Attic list allows 60 years between the destruction of Troy and the Return of the Heracleids, Eratosthenes allowed 80, putting the date of the Return in 1103 B.C. In this, however, he contradicts the Attic list, even as he has arranged it. The date of Melanthus is put 24 years before the return of the Heracleids, whereas it was the conquests of the Dorians in the Peloponnesus, which caused Melanthus and the Neleids of Pylus to seek refuge in Athens.

IX.

CRETAN KINGS.

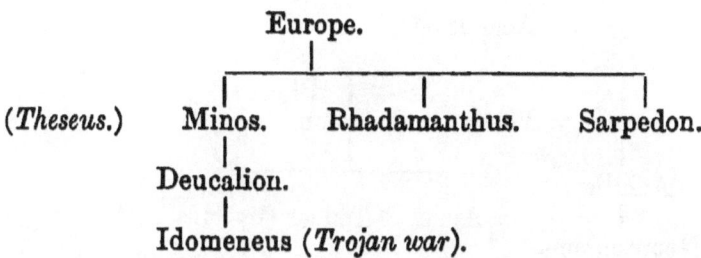

In the Iliad, Sarpedon has no connection with Crete, and is not the son of Europe.

The genealogy was invented after the Dorian colonisation of Crete, and is perhaps also intended to mark the connection between the Carians of Crete and the Carians of the mainland (through Sarpedon).

X.

AEACIDS.

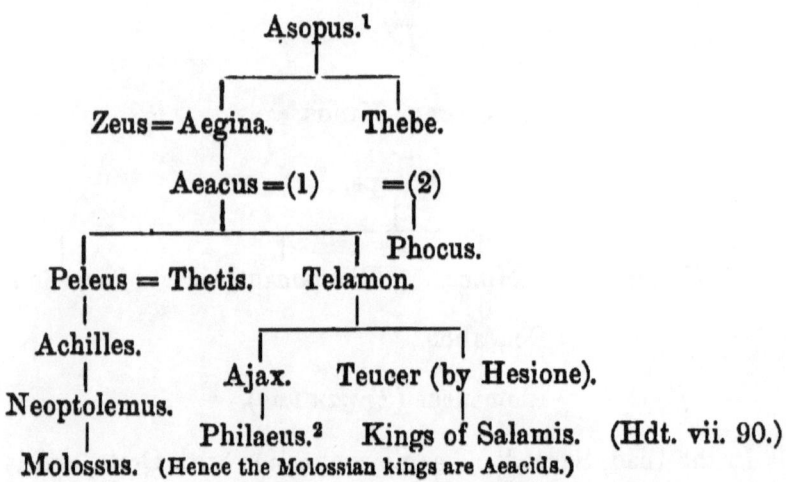

Peleus and Telamon, having slain their half brother Phocus, were compelled to leave Aegina. Peleus retired to Phthia; Telamon to Salamis. This genealogy therefore connects Aegina, Phthia, Salamis, Cyprus, and the Molossians of Epirus. Thebe and Aegina being sisters, the Thebans can apply to the Aeginetans as their next-of-kin (Hdt. v. 81, Ol. 68). For Aeacus and the Aeacidae, see Pind. Ol. viii. 41; Nem. v. 15; Ol. ii. 75 ff.; Isthm. vii. 40; Isthm. v. 30 ff.; Nem. iv. 50 ff.; Ol. ix. 74.

Grote, i. c. 10.

---

[1] There were two rivers named Asopus in Greece, one in Boeotia, the other near Sicyon.

[2] The Philaidae were an Attic gens.

XI.

KINGS OF THEBES.

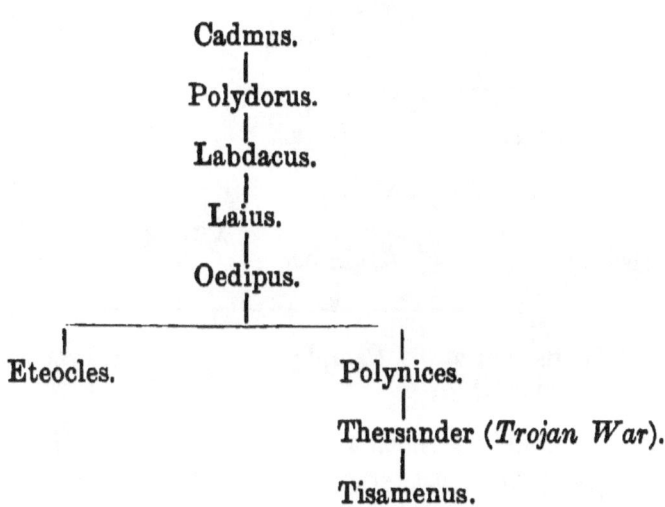

Herodotus (ii. 59) makes Laius contemporary with Amphitryon, which would make Heracles contemporary with Oedipus, *i.e.* two generations before the Trojan war. (Similarly in ii. 146, Heracles is 100 years before Pan, who is the son of Penelope.) But in ii. 145, Herodotus gives 1600 years before his own time as the date of Dionysus (*i.e.* 2050 B.C.) (according to the Theban legend, Dionysus is the son of Semele, the daughter of Cadmus), and 900 years before his own time as the date of Heracles. According to the first reckoning we have five generations = 166 years between Cadmus and Heracles, according to the second we have 700 years between Heracles and the grandson of Cadmus!

XII.

The Hellenes.

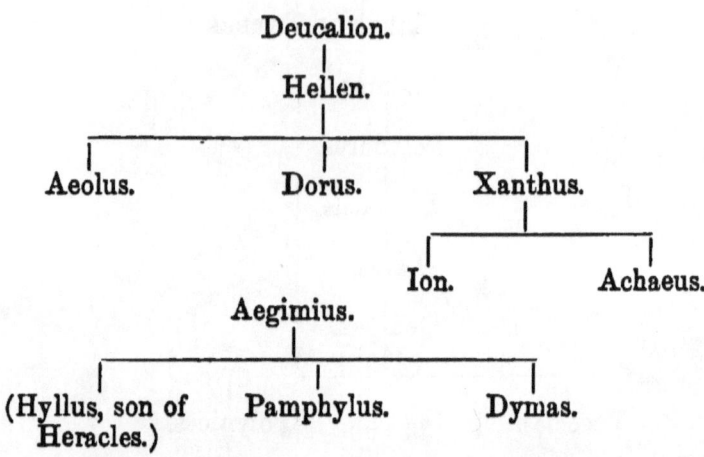

This is merely a scheme for bringing all the Greeks into relationship, and justifying the universal use of the word Hellenes. It could not therefore have been invented till the name Hellenes had become the name of all the Greeks. Dorus is sometimes said to be the father of Aegimius, but this relationship is doubtful. Aegimius adopted Hyllus, the son of Heracles, thus becoming the ancestor of the three Dorian tribes (Hylleis, Pamphyli, Dymanes), but the Hylleis alone are Heracleids. The Heracleid kings of Sparta claimed to be Achaeans (Hdt. v. 72). Cleomenes, when told by the priestess that no Dorian can enter the temple at Athens, replies—
οὐ Δωριεύς εἰμι ἀλλ' Ἀχαιός.

XIII.A.[1]

Kings of Macedonia.

(1. Caranus.)
(2. Coenus.)
(3. Thurimas.)
4. Perdiccas I.
5. Argaeus.
6. Philippus I.
7. Aeropus.

	Years.	B.C.
8. Alcetas.		
9. Amyntas I.,		(540)
10. Alexander I.,		(500)
11. Perdiccas II.,		(454)
12. Archelaus,	14	413
13. Orestes and Aeropus,	5	399
14. Pausanias,	1	394
15. Amyntas II.,	24	393
16. Alexander II.,	2	369
Ptolemaeus Alorites,	3	367
17. Perdiccas III.,	5	364
18. Philippus II.,	23	359
19. Alexander III.,	13	336
20. Philippus III., Aridaeus,	7	323
21. Cassander, ,	19	315
22. Philippus IV.,	(1)	296
23. Demetrius Poliorcetes,	7	294
24. Pyrrhus,	7 m.	287
25. Lysimachus,	5 y. 6 m. 3	286

(*Anarchy.*)

26. Antigonus Gonatas,	44	283
27. Demetrius II.,	10	239
28. Antigonus Doson,	9	229
29. Philippus V.,	42	220
30. Perseus,	11	178

[1] From Clinton's *Fasti Hellenici.*

XIII.B.—DETAILS OF THE LATER KINGS.[1]

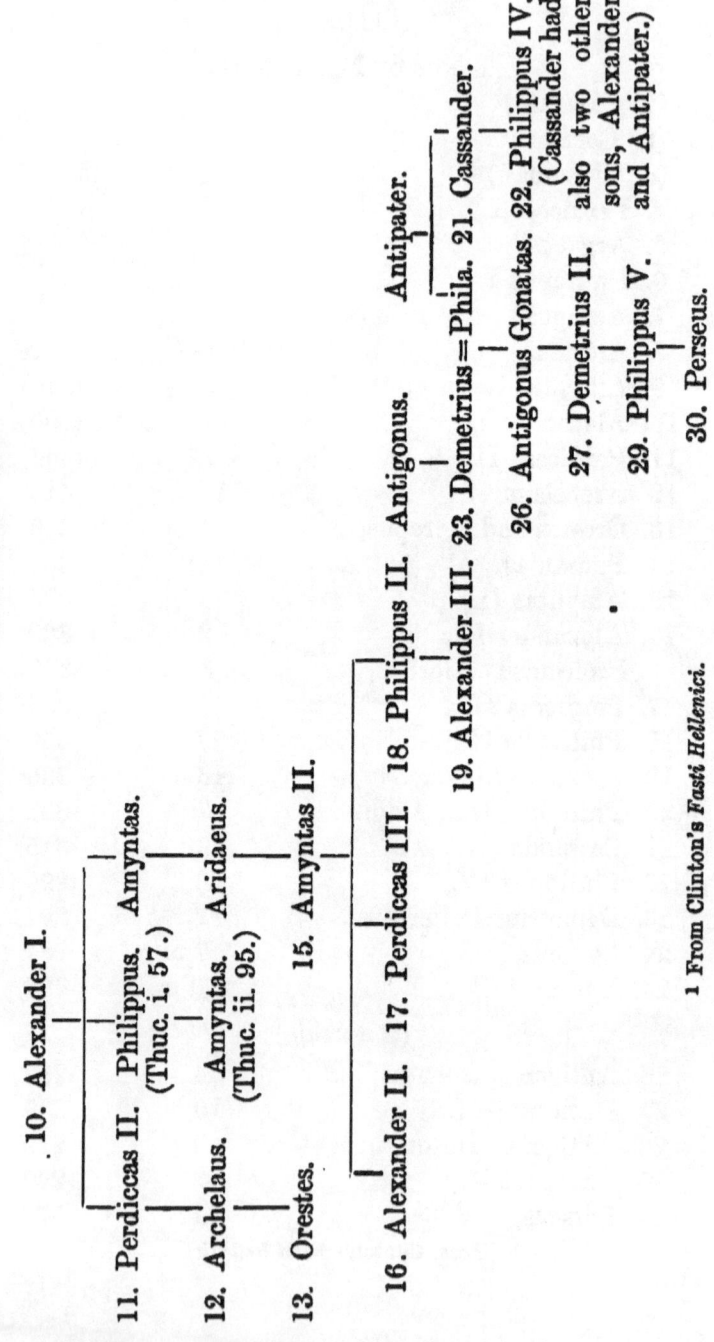

[1] From Clinton's *Fasti Hellenici*.

XIV.

Second Assyrian Empire.

	B.C.
Shalmanesar IV.,	780-770
Assurdanil II.,	770-752
Assurnivari,	752-745
Tiglath-Pilesar II.,	745-726
Shalmanesar V.,	726-721
Sargon,	721-704
Sennacherib,	704-681
Esarhaddon,	681-667
Assurbanipal,	667 ...
Assuridilani,	... 625

or, according to other accounts—

Assurbanipal,	667-625
Assuridilani,	625-606

See Duncker's *History of Antiquity*, iii. 291.

Maspero, *Histoire Ancienne*, p. 476.

XV.

Kings of Egypt.

Ethiopian Kings.

Sabakon.
|
Sevechus.
|
Tirhaka.
|
Urdamane.

During this period Assyria gains the ascendency over Egypt; in 663 B.C. Thebes is sacked by Esarhaddon, and a number of dynasts are set up in the place of the Ethiopian monarchs. Among these were Necho and his son Psammetichus, who succeeded in recovering the independence of their country.

Psammetichus I., . . . B.C. 664-610
|
Necho I., ... 610-595
|
Psammetichus II., ... 595-589
|
Apries (Hophrah), ... 589-570
|
Amasis, ... 570-526
|
Psammenitus, ... 526-525

Conquest of Egypt by Cambyses in 525 B.C.

XVI.

Lydian Kings.

A.

22 Heracleids = 505 years.

Gyges,	B.C. 716	38 years.
Ardys,	678	49 ,,
Sadyattes,	629	12 ,,
Alyattes,	617	57 ,,
Croesus,	560	14 ,,

Destruction of Sardis, 546 B.C.

The dates given by Eusebius do not agree with these dates of Herodotus. Cf. Duncker, *Hist. Ant.* iii. 170, 415, who arranges the reigns thus :—

B.

5 Mermnadae.

Gyges,	689-653
Ardys,	653-617
Sadyattes,	617-612
Alyattes,	612-563
Croesus,	563-549

fixing the date of the capture of Sardis before the burning of the temple of Delphi in 548 B.C.

XVII.

KINGS OF MEDIA.

	B.C.		
Deioces,	709	53 years	⎫ =75.
Phraortes,	656	22 „	⎭
Cyaxares,	634	40 „	⎫ =75.
Astyages,	594	35 „	⎭

Astyages was conquered by Cyrus in 559 B.C.

The total length of the Median monarchy is thus 150 years, but though Herodotus gives us these numbers for the various reigns, he fixes the total length of the empire at 128 years (i. 130).

Aeschylus (*Persae*, 756 ff.) speaks of two Median kings only :—

> Μῆδος γὰρ ἦν ὁ πρῶτος ἡγεμὼν στρατοῦ·
> ἄλλος δ' ἐκείνου παῖς τόδ' ἔργον ἤνυσεν.
>
> . . . . .
>
> τρίτος δ' ἀπ' αὐτοῦ Κῦρος.

And, in fact, the greatness of the Median empire appears to date from Cyaxares.

XVIII.

SECOND BABYLONIAN EMPIRE.

Nabopolassar,	625-605
Nebuchadnezzar,	605-561
Evilmerodach,	561-559
Neriglissar,	559-555
Bel labar iskun (*Labaessoarach*)	555 (for 9 months)
Nabonetus,	555-538

In 538 Cyrus captured Babylon.

See Duncker's *History of Antiquity*, iii. cc. 14, 15.
Maspero, *Histoire Ancienne*, p. 520.

XIX.

ATHENIAN FAMILIES.

(1.) *The Alcmaeonids.*

Megacles (archon in the time of the Cylonian affair).

Cleisthenes (of Sicyon).   Alcmaeon (friend of Croesus, Hdt. vi. 125).

Megacles = Agariste.

├── Cleisthenes of Athens.
│   └── Megacles.
│   └── Dinomache = Clinias.
│   └── Alcibiades.
└── Hippocrates.
    ├── Megacles.
    │   └── Euryptolemus.
    │   └── Isodice = Cimon.
    └── Agariste. (Hdt. vi. 131.)
        └── Pericles.

(2.) *The Family of Militiades.*

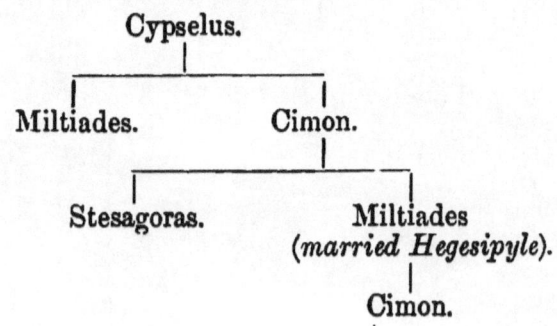

Cypselus.
├── Miltiades.
└── Cimon.
    ├── Stesagoras.
    └── Miltiades (*married Hegesipyle*).
        └── Cimon.

XX.

ATHENIAN ARCHONS.

(1.) *For Ten Years.*

Charops,	Ol. 7. 1.	752 B.C.
Aesimides,	Ol. 9. 3.	742
Clidicus,	Ol. 12. 1.	732
Hippomenes,	Ol. 14. 3.	722
Leocrates,	Ol. 17. 1.	712
Apsander,	Ol. 19. 3.	702
Eryxias,	Ol. 22. 1.	692

(2.) *For One Year.*

B.C.	OL.		B.C.	OL.	
682.	24.3.	Creon.	590.	47.3.	Simon.
681.	24.4.	Tlesias.	588.	48.1.	Philippus.
671.	27.2.	Leostratus.	585.	48.4.	Damasias I ?
669.	27.4.	Peisistratus	582.	49.3.	Damasias II.
668.	28.1.	Autosthenes	577.	50.4.	Archestratides.
664.	29.1.	Miltiades.	570.	52.3.	Aristomenes.
659.	30.2.	Miltiades.	566.	53.3.	Hippocleides.
644.	34.1.	Dropides.	560.	55.1.	Comias.
639.	35.2.	Damasias.	559.	55.2.	Hegestratus.
621.	39.4.	Dracon.	556.	56.1.	Euthydemus.
615.	41.2.	Heniochides.	548.	58.1.	Erxicleides.
605.	43.4.	Aristocles.	536.	61.1.	………naeus.
604.	44.1.	Critias.	533.	61.4.	Thericles.
599.	45.2.	Megacles.	524.	64.1.	Miltiades.
595.	46.2.	Philombrotus.	508.	68.1.	Isagoras.
594.	46.3.	Solon.	504.	69.1.	Acestorides.
593.	46.4.	Dropides.	500.	70.1.	Myrus.
592.	47.1.	Eucrates.	496.	71.1.	Hipparchus.

B.C.	OL.		B.C.	OL.	
495.	71.2.	Philippus.	462.	79.3.	Conon.
494.	71.3.	Pythocritus.	461.	79.4.	Euthippus.
493.	71.4.	Themistocles.	460.	80.1.	Phrasicleides.
492.	72.1.	Diognetus.	459.	80.2.	Philocles.
491.	72.2.	Hybrilides.	458.	80.3.	Bion.
490.	72.3.	Phaenippus.	457.	80.4.	Mnesitheides.
489.	72.4.	Aristeides.	456.	81.1.	Callias.
488.	73.1.	Anchises.	455.	81.2.	Sosistratus.
485.	73.4.	Philocrates.	454.	81.3.	Ariston.
484.	74.1.	Leostratus.	453.	81.4.	Lysicrates.
483.	74.2.	Nicodemus.	452.	82.1.	Chaerephanes.
482.	74.3.	Themistocles.	451.	82.2.	Antidotus.
480.	75.1.	Calliades.	450.	82.3.	Euthydemus.
479.	75.2.	Xanthippus.	449.	82.4.	Pedieus.
478.	75.3.	Timosthenes.	448.	83.1.	Philiscus.
477.	75.4.	Adeimantus.	447.	83.2.	Timarchides.
476.	76.1.	Phaedon.	446.	83.3.	Callimachus.
475.	76.2.	Dromocleides.	445.	83.4.	Lysimachides.
474.	76.3.	Acestorides.	444.	84.1.	Praxiteles.
473.	76.4.	Menon.	443.	84.2.	Lysanias.
472.	77.1.	Chares.	442.	84.3.	Diphilus.
471.	77.2.	Praxiergus.	441.	84.4.	Timocles.
470.	77.3.	Demotion.	440.	85.1.	Morychides.
469.	77.4.	Apsephion.	439.	85.2.	Glaucinus.
468.	78.1.	Theagenides.	438.	85.3.	Theodorus.
467.	78.2.	Lysistratus.	437.	85.4.	Euthymenes.
466.	78.3.	Lysanias.	436.	86.1.	Lysimachus.
465.	78.4.	Lysitheus.	435.	86.2.	Antiochides.
464.	79.1.	Archedemides.	434.	86.3.	Crates.
463.	79.2.	Tlepolemus.	433.	86.4.	Apseudes.

ATHENIAN ARCHONS.

B.C.	OL.		B.C.	OL.	
432.	87.1.	Pythodorus.	402.	94.3.	Micon.
431.	87.2.	Euthydemus.	401.	94.4.	Xenaenetus.
430.	87.3.	Apollodorus.	400.	95.1.	Laches.
429.	87.4.	Epameinon.	399.	95.2.	Aristocrates.
428.	88.1.	Diotimus.	398.	95.3.	Ithycles.
427.	88.2.	Eucles.	397.	95.4.	Suniades.
426.	88.3.	Euthynus.	396.	96.1.	Phormion.
425.	88.4.	Stratocles.	395.	96.2.	Diophantus.
424.	89.1.	Isarchus.	394.	96.3.	Eubulides.
423.	89.2.	Amynias.	393.	96.4.	Demostratus.
422.	89.3.	Alcaeus.	392.	97.1.	Philocles.
421.	89.4.	Aristion.	391.	97.2.	Nicoteles.
420.	90.4.	Astyphilus.	390.	97.3.	Demostratus.
419.	90.2.	Archias.	389.	97.4.	Antipater.
418.	90.3.	Antiphon.	388.	98.1.	Pyrgius.
417.	90.4.	Euphemus.	387.	98.2.	Theodotus.
416.	91.1.	Arimnestus.	386.	98.3.	Mystichides.
415.	91.2.	Chabrias.	385.	98.4.	Dexitheus.
414.	91.3.	Tisander.	384.	99.1.	Diotrephes.
413.	91.4.	Cleocritus.	383.	99.2.	Phanostratus.
412.	92.1.	Callias.	382.	99.3.	Evander.
411.	92.2.	Theopompus.	381.	99.4.	Demophilus.
410.	92.3.	Glaucippus.	380.	100.1.	Pytheas.
409.	92.4.	Diocles.	379.	100.2.	Nicon.
408.	93.1.	Euctemon.	378.	100.3.	Nausinicus.
407.	93.2.	Antigenes.	377.	100.4.	Calleas.
406.	93.3.	Callias.	376.	101.1.	Charisander.
405.	93.4.	Alexias.	375.	101.2.	Hippodamas.
404.	94.1.	*Anarchia.*	374.	101.3.	Socratides.
403.	94.2.	Eucleides.	373.	101.4.	Asteius.

ATHENIAN ARCHONS.

B.C.	OL.		B.C.	OL.	
372.	102.1.	Alcisthenes.	346.	108.3.	Archias.
371.	102.2.	Phrasicleides.	345.	108.4.	Eubulus.
370.	102.3.	Dysnicetus.	344.	109.1.	Lyciscus.
369.	102.4.	Lysistratus.	343.	109.2.	Pythodotus.
368.	103.1.	Nausigenes.	342.	109.3.	Sosigenes.
367.	103.2.	Polyzelus.	341.	109.4.	Nicomachus.
366.	103.3.	Cephisodorus.	340.	110.1.	Theophrastus.
365.	103.4.	Chion.	339.	110.2.	Lysimachides.
364.	104.1.	Timocrates.	338.	110.3.	Chaerondas.
363.	104.2.	Charicleides.	337.	110.4.	Phrynichus.
362.	104.3.	Molon.	336.	111.1.	Pythodelus.
361.	104.4.	Nicophemus.	335.	111.2.	Euaenetus.
360.	105.1.	Kallimedes.	334.	111.3.	Ctesicles.
359.	105.2.	Eucharistus.	333.	111.4.	Nicocrates.
358.	105.3.	Cephisodotus.	332.	112.1.	Nicetes.
357.	105.4.	Agathocles.	331.	112.2.	Aristophanes.
356.	106.1.	Elpines.	330.	112.3.	Aristophon.
355.	106.2.	Callistratus.	329.	112.4.	Cephisophon.
354.	106.3.	Diotimus.	328.	113.1.	Euthycritus.
353.	106.4.	Thudemus.	327.	113.2.	Hegemon.
352.	107.1.	Aristodemus.	326.	113.3.	Chremes.
351.	107.2.	Thessalus.	325.	113.4.	Anticles.
350.	107.3.	Apollodorus.	324.	114.1.	Hegesias.
349.	107.4.	Callimachus.	323.	114.2.	Cephisodorus.
348.	108.1.	Theophilus.	322.	114.3.	Philocles.
347.	108.2.	Themistocles.	321.	114.4.	Archippus.

Before 496 our knowledge of the Athenian Archons is very defective. From 496 to 321 we have a complete list, with the exception of 487, 486, and 481 B.C.

XXI.

LIST OF VICTORS IN THE STADIUM OR FOOT-RACE AT OLYMPIA.

We possess a list of the victors at Olympia from 776 B.C. to 221 A.D. It has been copied by Eusebius from Julius Africanus, who flourished in Palestine in the reign of Elagabalus (218-222). Africanus, of course, copied from still earlier lists, adding to them the victors down to his own time.

These lists appear to have been kept by the Hellenodikai, or umpires of the games (Paus. vi. 8, 1). They are often quoted by Pausanias as the records of the Eleans touching the Olympian victors τὰ 'Ηλείων ἐς τοὺς 'Ολυμπιονίκας γράμματα (Paus. iii. 21, 1; v. 21, 9; vi. 2, 3, 13, 10,) who also informs us that the names had been preserved continuously from the time of Coroebus (v. 8, 4; 24, 5), and that they were written in the gymnasium at Olympia by a certain Paraballon (vi. 6, 3). The first to publish a list was Hippias of Elis, whose work is blamed for its inaccuracy by Plutarch, *Num. init.* (Cf. S. Julii Africani 'Ολυμπιάδων ἀναγραφή : ed. Rutgers.)

OL.	B.C.	
1.	776.	Coroebus, an Elean.
2.	772.	Antimachus, an Elean.
3.	768.	Androclus, a Messenian.
4.	764.	Polychares, a Messenian.
5.	760.	Aeschines, an Elean.
6.	756.	Oebotas, a Dymean.
7.	752.	Daïcles, a Messenian.
8.	748.	Anticles, a Messenian.
9.	744.	Xenocles, a Messenian.
10.	740.	Dotadas, a Messenian.
11.	736.	Leochares, a Messenian.

OL.	B.C.	
12.	732.	Oxythemis, a Cleonean.
13.	728.	Diocles, a Corinthian.
14.	724.	Desmon, a Corinthian.

The diaulos was now added.

15.	720.	Orsippus, a Megarian.

The dolichus was added and the runners discontinued the girdle.

16.	716.	Pythagoras, a Lacedaemonian.
17.	712.	Polus, an Epidaurian.
18.	708.	Tellis, a Sicyonian.

The wrestling and the Pentathlon were added.

19.	704.	Menus, a Megarian.
20.	700.	Atheradas, a Laconian.
21.	696.	Pantacles, an Athenian.
22.	692.	Pantacles *again*.
23.	688.	Icarius, a Hyperasian.

The boxing was now added.

24.	684.	Cleoptolemus, a Laconian.
25.	680.	Thalpius, a Laconian.

The four-horse race was added.

26.	676.	Callisthenes, a Laconian.
27.	672.	Eurybates, an Athenian.
28.	668.	Charmis, a Laconian.

This Olympiad was held by the Pisaeans, the Eleans being at war with Dyme.

29.	664.	Chionis, a Laconian.
30.	660.	Chionis *again*.

The Pisaeans held this Olympiad independently, and the following twenty-two.

31.	656.	Chionis *again*.

OLYMPIAN VICTORS.

OL.	B.C.	
32.	652.	Cratinus, a Megarian.
33.	648.	Gyges, a Laconian.
		The Pancratium was now added, and the horse race.
34.	644.	Stomas, an Athenian.
35.	640.	Sphaerus, a Laconian.
36.	636.	Arytamas, a Laconian.
37.	632.	Euryclidas, a Laconian.
		The foot race and wrestling for boys added.
38.	628.	Olyntheus, a Laconian.
		The pentathlon for boys introduced, but it was not continued.
39.	624.	Rhipsolaus, a Laconian.
40.	620.	Olyntheus, a Laconian *again*.
41.	661.	Cleondas, a Theban.
		Boxing for the boys added.
42.	612.	Lycotas, a Laconian.
43.	608.	Cleon, an Epidaurian.
44.	604.	Gelon, a Laconian.
45.	600.	Anticrates, an Epidaurian.
46.	596.	Chrysomachus, a Laconian.
47.	592.	Eurycles, a Laconian.
48.	588.	Glycon, a Crotoniate.
49.	584.	Lycinus, a Crotoniate.
50.	580.	Epitelidas, a Laconian.
51.	576.	Eratosthenes, a Crotoniate.
52.	572.	Agis, an Elean.
53.	568.	Hagnon, a Peparethian.
54.	564.	Hippostratus, a Crotoniate.
55.	560.	Hippostratus *again*.

OLYMPIAN VICTORS.

OL.	B.C.	
56.	556.	Phaedrus, a Pharsalian.
57.	552.	Ladromus, a Laconian.
58.	548.	Diognetus, a Crotoniate.
59.	544.	Archilochus, a Corcyrean.
60.	540.	Apellaeus, an Elean.
61.	536.	Agatharchus, a Corcyrean.
62.	532.	Eryxias, a Chalcidian.

  At this time Milo conquered in the wrestling. He was victor six times at the Olympia, six at the Pythia, ten at the Isthmia, and nine at the Nemea.

  Cimon, the Athenian, was victorious in the chariot race.

63.	528.	Parmenides, a Camarinean.

  Pisistratus victorious in the chariot race.

64.	524.	Menander, a Thessalian.

  Cimon was again victorious in the chariot race.

65.	520.	Anochus, a Tarentine.

  The race in armour was added.

66.	516.	Ischyrus, a Himeraean.
67.	512.	Phanas, a Pellenaean.
68.	508.	Isomachus, a Crotoniate.
69.	504.	Isomachus *again*.
70.	500.	Niceas, an Opuntian.

  The mule race added.

71.	496.	Tisicrates, a Crotoniate.
72.	492.	Tisicrates *again*.
73.	488.	Aslytus, a Crotoniate.

  Gelon victorious in the chariot race. Hiero victorious in the horse race.

OL.	B.C.	
74.	484.	Aslytus *again*.
75.	480.	Aslytus *again*.
76.	476.	Scamandrius, a Mytilenean.
77.	472.	Dandes, an Argive.
		Hiero victorious in the horse race.
78.	468.	Parmenides, a Poseidoniate.
		Hiero victorious in the chariot race.
79.	464.	Xenophon, a Corinthian.
80.	460.	Torymmas, a Thessalian.
		Arcesilaus of Cyrene victorious in the chariot race.
81.	456.	Polymnestus, a Cyrenean.
82.	452.	Lycus, a Larisaean.
		Psaumis of Camarina was victorious with the mules.
83.	448.	Crison, a Himeraean.
84.	444.	Crison *again*.
		The mule race is discontinued.
85.	440.	Crison *again*.
86.	436.	Theopompus, a Thessalian.
87.	432.	Sophron, an Ambraciote.
88.	428.	Symmachus, a Messenian.
89.	424.	Symmachus *again*.
90.	420.	Hyperbius, a Syracusan.
91.	416.	Exaenetus, an Agrigentine.
		Alcibiades is victorious with the chariot race.
92.	412.	Exaenetus *again*.
93.	408.	Eubotas, a Cyrenean.
		The race with the pair of horses added.
94.	404.	Crocinas, a Larisaean.

OL.	B.C.	
95.	400.	Minos, an Athenian.
96.	396.	Eupolemus, an Elean.
		The contests for trumpeters and heralds added.
97.	392.	Terinaeus, an Elean.
98.	388.	Sosippus, a Delphian.
99.	384.	Dicon, a Syracusan.
		The chariot race for young horses added.
100.	386.	Dionysodorus, a Tarentine.
101.	376.	Damon, a Thurian.
102.	372.	Damon *again*.
103.	368.	Pythostratus, an Ephesian.
104.	364.	Phocides, an Athenian.
		This Olympiad was held by the Pisaeans.
105.	360.	Porus, a Cyrenean.
106.	356.	Porus *again*.
107.	352.	Micrinas, a Tarentine.
108.	348.	Polycles, a Cyrenean.
109.	344.	Aristolochus, an Athenian.
110.	340.	Anticles, an Athenian.
111.	336.	Cleomantis, a Cleitorian.
112.	332.	Gryllus, a Chalcidian.
113.	328.	Cliton, a Macedonian.
114.	324.	Micinas, a Rhodian.'
115.	320.	Damasias, an Amphipolitan.

PART II.

CHRONOLOGICAL TABLES

CHRONOLOGICAL TABLES.

I.

FROM THE TROJAN WAR TO THE FIRST OLYMPIAD.

B.C.	
1183.	FALL OF TROY (*see note*).
1133.	The Thessalians, issuing from Thesprotia, invade Thessaly. (Duncker, *Hist. of Greece*, bk. ii. c. 1; Curtius, i. 155; Grote, pt. i. c. 18. sect. 2.)
1123.	The Arnaeans are driven from Thessaly into Boeotia (Cadmeis). (Hdt. vii. 176; Thuc. i. 13.)
1103.	**The Dorians invade the Peloponnese.** Temenus, Aristodemus, Cresphontes. (Grote, i. c. 18, sect. 1. Thuc. i. 13.)
1074.	About this time the **Dorians** in the Peloponnesus obtain possession of **Corinth, Sicyon, Troezen, Epidaurus and Aegina.** The old population is either expelled or amalgamated. (Curtius, i. p. 171; Grote, i. 18, sect. 1.)
	Thera colonised. (Hdt. iv. 146-149; Duncker, bk. ii. c. 11; Grote, i. 18, sect. 3, 3.)
1066.	**Megara** passes into the hands of the Dorians (Hdt. v. 76), who also colonise **Melos** (Thuc. v. 112), **Cnidus, Halicarnassus** from Troezen (Hdt. vii. 99), **Rhodes** and a large part of **Crete** (Duncker, bk. ii., cc. 7, 11).
	At Athens, about this time, **Codrus is slain in battle against the Dorians.** The monarchy comes to an end, and life archons are established. (Grote, i. 18; Duncker, bk. ii. c. 3.)

B.C.	
1054.	**Foundation of the Aeolian colonies in Asia Minor**—Lesbos, 1053; Cyme, 1033; Smyrna, 1015 (Grote, i. 18). These dates are traditional; Jerome puts Cyme 1048 B.C., and Smyrna 1046 B.C. They are probably from 50 to 100 years too early (Duncker, bk. ii. c. 2).
1044.	**The sons of Codrus lead out colonies into Asia Minor.** (These colonies also are too early at this date. Duncker, bk. i. c. 4, puts them after the Aeolian *i.e.* Achaean colonies, about 950 B.C.)
996.	Labotas, king of Sparta; **this is the earliest date for Lycurgus.**
950.	*Possible date of the Homeric poems.* (The date cannot be fixed precisely, for there are older and later elements in the poems. Herodotus puts Homer and Hesiod 400 years before his own time, and no more. This would give 850 B.C. From the limited knowledge of geography in Homer, the poems must have been composed before the voyage of the Milesians into the Black Sea, about 800 B.C. On the other hand, the Dorians were in Crete when the poems were composed (Idomeneus), and this gives an upward limit of 900 B.C., for the Dorians were not in Crete till after their occupation of the Peloponnese. The Odyssey must be before 750 B.C., the date at which Sicily and the west became known to the Greeks, but subsequent to the Iliad, from which it has borrowed the legend of Idomeneus and the Cretans (*Od.* xix. 170 ff.). The catalogue is later, about 650 B.C. (Cf. Duncker, bk. i. c. 12.)
884.	Charilaus, king of Sparta, **later date of Lycurgus.** *Hesiodic poetry.*

NOTE ON THE DATE OF THE TROJAN WAR.

The date given in the table is that of Eratosthenes, who allows 860 years between the taking of Troy and the death of Alexander the Great; 860 + 323 = 1183 B.C. (Clemens Alex., *Strom.* i. 21, sec. 138). Eratosthenes founded his computation on the list of the Spartan kings (Plutarch, *Lycurg.* i.) in which the first Olympiad was placed in the tenth year of Alcamenes and Theopompus. Before Alcamenes we have nine names of Agiad kings, counting Eurystheus and including Menelaus; before Theopompus we have eight names of Eurypontids, including the regency of Lycurgus. The interval between the first Olympiad and the return of the Heracleids in this list is 327 years, and if from this we deduct 10 years for the reigns of Alcamenes and Theopompus, we have 317 years for the nine Agiads and the eight Eurypontids. This gives an average of much more than thirty years for each reign; in fact, for the Eurypontids the average is nearly 40 years. Such an average would be excessive even for generations, and is very doubtful for reigns. From the Conquest to the present time we have thirty-five sovereigns in English history (excluding the eleven years of the Commonwealth) in 800 years, which gives an average of a little less than 23 years for a reign, a length which is almost identical with the average which Herodotus gives (i. 7) for the Lydian kings of the Heracleid dynasty (505 years for 22 "generations" = 23 years for each, nearly). Even since the accession of George I., notwithstanding the long reigns of George III. and Victoria, the average length of a reign has been only twenty-four years, and it is not likely that this length would be exceeded in a time of disturbance, when the kings were leaders of their armies.

For this reason it is probable that the date of the Trojan war was placed too high by Eratosthenes. If we assume eight reigns at Sparta before the first Olympiad, and allow 25 years for a reign, we reach the total of 200 years for the interval between 776 B.C. and the return of the Heracleids. This will put the Return, or in other words, the establishment of the Dorians in the Peloponnese, at 1000 B.C. in round numbers, so that the fall of Troy, which on the computation of Eratosthenes preceded the Return by 80 years, will be put at 1080 B.C.

Other dates are given by Isocrates, Ephorus, and Democritus, which range from 33 to 63 years later than 1183 (Clinton, *Fasti Hellenici*, ii. 5). Phanias of Eresus put the date 55 years later; Callimachus, 56 years later, allowing only 14 Olympiads between Iphitus and Coroebus, and not, as Eratosthenes, 27 Olympiads (= 108 years).

On the other hand, the date given in the "Parian Marble" for the fall of Troy is 26 years *above* that of Eratosthenes— 1209 B.C. In the marble also, which seems to preserve a computation founded on the lists of the Attic kings, the interval between the fall of Troy and the Return of the Heracleids is not 80, but 60 years.

Herodotus does not fix the era of the fall of Troy, but we can fix it from dates which he supplies. In ii. 145 he tells us that Pan, who was supposed to be the son of Penelope and Hermes, lived after the Trojan war, and about 800 years before his own time. If we suppose Herodotus to have been 30 in 454 B.C., $454 + 800$ ($=1254$) is a date somewhat later than the Trojan war. This date seems to be founded on Lydian annals. The Heracleid dynasty of Sardis fell in 716 B.C.; it lasted 505 years, and the founder was fifth in descent from Heracles (4 generations $= 133$ years). But $716 + 505 + 133 = 1354$ as the date of Heracles, who is 100 years before Pan (Hdt. i. 7). On the other hand the Lacedaemonian lists quoted by Herodotus (vii. 204), which give 20 generations from the Return to Leonidas, do not agree with this date (Leonidas fell 480 B.C. and 20 generations $= 666$ years; $480 + 666 = 1146$ as the date of the Return).

The Dorian invasion of Peloponnesus is a distinct historical fact, which brought about a change in the reigning families of the cities which they occupied. When, therefore, we find eight generations, more or less, in Sparta, Arcadia, and Corinth, for the interval between the first Olympiad and the Dorian occupation of the cities, we may fairly assume that some great political change took place in Peloponnesus about the year 1000 B.C. This calculation makes it necessary to bring down the traditional dates for the colonisation of the islands of the Aegean and of Asia Minor by about a century. For it was in consequence of the disturbance caused by the Dorians that the Achaean (Aeolian) and Ionian colonists left the shores of Greece; and the Dorians did not begin to colonise the islands till they were themselves established in the Peloponnesus.

Note on the Date of Lycurgus.

Thucydides considers that 400 years and more elapsed between the time that the Lacedaemonians enjoyed good government and the end of the Peloponnesian war. This, if we suppose that the reference is to the constitution of Lycurgus, from which Herodotus dates the prosperity of the Lacedaemonians, would give a date of about 800 for Lycurgus. With this agrees the legend which connects Lycurgus with Iphitus and the renewal of the Olympic games.

CHRONOLOGICAL TABLES.

II.

FROM 776 TO 323 B.C.

B.C.	Olympiad	
776.	1.1.	**Victory of Coroebus in the Olympic games.** *Arctinus the Epic poet.* The year of the beginning of the Peloponnesian war is fixed by the eclipse of the sun in 431 B.C. (Thuc. ii. 28), and Eratosthenes (in Clemens Alex., *Strom.* i. p. 336) gives 345 years from the first year in Ol. 1. to the Peloponnesian war (345+431=776 for the year in which Ol. 1. 1. began). The first Olympiad took place in the second year of Aeschylus, life-archon at Athens, and in the tenth year of Alcamenes and Theopompus, kings of Sparta. *Arctinus of Miletus is placed at this date (or one year later) on the authority of Eusebius. He was the reputed author of the "Aethiopis" in four books, and the* Ἰλίου πέρσις *in two books* (Kinkel, *Epic. Graec. Frag.*, pp. 33 ff., 49 ff.).
765.	2 3.	**Sinope** founded by Miletus. It was founded before the invasion of the Cimmerians in 750 B.C., and refounded after being destroyed in 632 B.C. (Duncker, *Hist. Ant.* i. 545).
765.	3.4.	*Cinaethon of Lacedaemon.* (*Epic poet.*) *He was the author of the "Telegonia" and a poem on Oedipus. His works were extant in the time of Pausanias (second cent. A.D.) who speaks of them as genealogies, Paus. ii. 3. 7:* Κιναίθων ὁ Λακεδαιμόνιος, ἐγενεαλόγησε γὰρ καὶ οὗτος ἔπεσι. *ib.* iv. 2, 1: ὁπόσα Κιναίθων ἐγενεαλόγησε. (Cp. Kinkel, *Epic. Graec. Frag.*, p. 196.)
761.	4.4.	*Eumelus.* (*Epic poet.*) *He was a member of the Bacchiadae of Corinth. He is quoted by Pausanias on the antiquities of Corinth* ii. 1. 1.; ii. 3. 8. (Cp. Kinkel, *Epic. Graec. Frag.*, pp. 185-195). **Asine** conquered by the Argives.

B.C.	OL.	
757.	5.4.	**Trapezus founded by Sinope.** That Trapezus was a colony of Sinope we know from Xen. *Anab.* iv. 8. 22, etc. Other colonies of this city were Cotyora and Cerasus. Sinope was herself a colony of Miletus (Xen. *Anab.* v. 9. 15).
756.	6.1.	**Cyzicus founded by Miletus.** Cyzicus was subsequently recolonised by Megara (675 B.C.)
753.	6.4.	*Antimachus of Teus.* *He was an epic poet.* (Kinkel, *Ep. Graec. Frag.*, p. 247.) [This is the Varronian date for the foundation of Rome.]
752.	7.1.	**Decennial Archons at Athens.** Alcmaeon the last life-archon was deposed after a rule of two years. (Cp. Genealogies VIII., p. 30.)
750.	7.3.	This is the period of the greatest power of the Milesians, who are said to have founded no fewer than 80 colonies. (Curt. *Hist. Greece*, i. 422. Strabo, p. 635 : πολλὰ δὲ τῆς πόλεως ἔργα ταύτης, μέγιστον δὲ τὸ πλῆθος τῶν ἀποικιῶν. ὅ τε γὰρ Εὔξεινος πόντος ὑπὸ τούτων συνῴκισται πᾶς καὶ ἡ Προποντὶς και ἄλλοι πλείους τόποι.)
748.	8.1.	**Pheidon, king of Argos, with the Pisatans, drives out the Eleans and celebrates the Olympic festival in this year.** (Paus. vi. 22. 2.) Others put Pheidon three generations higher, making him a contemporary of Iphitus and Lycurgus. Others again bring him much lower (668 B.C., Curtius) on the strength of Hdt. vi. 127, where Leocedes, the son of Pheidon, is one of the suitors for Agariste, the daughter of Cleisthenes of Sicyon. (For Pheidon see Hdt. and Paus. *ll. cc.*; Plut. *Amator. Narr.* 2.) **He was the first to introduce a system of coinage, weights and measures into Greece** (the so-called Aeginetan standard).
745.	8.4.	**Automenes, king of Corinth, is deposed, and annual prytanies are set up in his place.** (Paus. ii. 44.)
745-726.		Tiglath-Pilesar II. is king of Assyria.
743.	9.2.	**Alcamenes and Theopompus, kings of Sparta; outbreak of the first Messenian War which lasted twenty years.** (Paus. iv. 5. 4.) [735-716, Duncker, *Hist. Greece*, bk. iii. c. 4.]

B.C.	OL.	
743.	9.2.	**Rhegium** founded by Chalcis. (The foundation took place in the Messenian War, for Strabo, p. 257, quotes Antiochus to the effect that Messenian exiles joined in it, and Messenians were leaders (ἡγεμόνες) of Rhegium down to the time of Anaxilaus.)
735.	11.2.	**Naxos** founded by Chalcis. (Thuc. vi. 3. Strabo, p. 267. Theocles the founder was an Athenian.)
734.	11.3.	**Syracuse founded by Archias of Corinth.** (Strab. 269.) He was exiled owing to the death of Actaeon. (Plut. *Amator. Narr.* 2.)
	11.4.	**Corcyra** colonised by the Corinthians, under Chersicrates, who expelled the Eretrians. (Strabo, 289.)
730.	12.3.	Leontini and Catana founded by Naxos. (Thuc. vi. 3 ; Strabo, 272.)
728.	13.1.	**Hyblaean Megara** founded by Megara. (Thuc. vi. 4. The Megarians had lived here 245 years before the city was captured by Gelon in 483 B.C. Strabo, p. 267.) *Philolaus, a Bacchiade of Corinth, gives laws to the Thebans.* (Arist. *Pol.* ii. 12.)
726-721.		Shalmanesar V., king of Assyria.
724.	14.1.	**Messenia conquered by the Spartans in the twentieth year of the war.** (Paus. iv. 13. 5, and for the length of the war, Tyrtaeus *frag.* 5, Bergk.)
721-704.		Sargon, king of Assyria.
721.	14.4.	**Sybaris** founded by the Achaeans of Peloponnesus. (Strabo, 263. Isus of Helice was the leader. Diodorus, xii. 9. Scymnus, 337 ff.) About this time (Candaules being king of Lydia) the Cimmerians invaded Asia Minor.
720.	15.1.	**Orsippus of Megara.** He was the first who ran at Olympia without a girdle. Rise of Megara into power. (C. I. G. 1050. Hicks, "*Manual,*" No. I.)
716.	16.1.	**Date of Gyges** king of Lydia, according to

B.C.	OL.	
715.	16.2.	Herodotus. *See* Genealogies XVI. p. 39. The date given by Assyrian documents is later. Abydus founded by Miletus. (In the reign of Gyges,—Strabo, 590.) *About this time we may place* Callinus *the Elegiac poet, who referred to the Magnesians before their overthrow by the Cimmerians (in the reign of Candaules of Lydia,* Pliny, *H. N.* 35. 8.), *and the conquest of Sardis by the Cimmerians.*
710.	17.3.	Croton founded by the Achaeans. They were led by Myscelus. (Dionys. Hal. *Ant.* ii. p. 361.)
709-656.	17.4.	Deioces, king of Media, according to Herodotus.
708.	18.1.	Parium founded by the Milesians, Erythraeans, and Parians. (Strabo, 589.) Tarentum founded by the Parthenii from Sparta. (Strabo, 231, 232.) About this time the Corinthians built triremes (Thuc. i. 13). Ameinocles at Samos. Thasos colonised by the Parians. (Telesicles and his son Archilochus take part in the colony.) (Strabo, 370; Paus. x. 28. 3.) This is placed in 720 B.C. by Curtius (after Dionysius).
704-681.		Sennacherib, king of Assyria.

700.	20.1.	About this time may be placed the poets
		  Archilochus *of Paros*, (*iambic*),
		  Simonides *of Amorgus*, (*iambic*).
		Archilochus was later than Callinus, *but lived in the reign of Gyges* (Hdt. i. 12). *He joined in the colony at Thasos, and became famous after the 20th Olympiad* (Clemens, *Strom.* i. p. 333).
		Simonides *is placed by Suidas 490 years after the Trojan war*—693 B.C.
		Perdiccas I., king of Macedonia.

693.	21.4.	Midas of Phrygia takes his life owing to the invasion of Phrygia by the Cimmerians (Eusebius).
690.	22.3.	Gela founded by Rhodes and Crete. (Thuc. vi. 4.) Phaselis in Lycia founded by the Dorians. (Hdt. ii. 178.)

B.C.	OL.	
687.	23.2.	Herodotus in his total sum (as opposed to the length of the separate reigns) puts the beginning of the Median Empire at this date (i. 130), 128 years before the fall, *i.e.* before 559 B.C.
685.	23.4.	Rebellion of the Messenians under Aristomenes. **Second Messenian War.** (Paus. iv. 15. 1.) The date is probably too high. Tyrtaeus, who lived during the Second War, speaks of the first as "waged by the fathers of our fathers," and Justin allows 80 years between the two wars. Nor is the length of the war certain. (645-628 B.C., Curtius; 645-631, Duncker.)
683.	24.2.	**Nine yearly archons** at Athens in place of one decennial archon. *Tyrtaeus came from Athens to Sparta in the Second Messenian War, and was admitted a citizen of Sparta. He was their general in the War. His poems were greatly prized at Sparta, and used in education.*
681-667.		Esarhaddon, king of Assyria.
678-629.	25.3.	Ardys, king of Lydia. (Hdt. i. 16.) (652-15 according to oriental dates).
676.	26.1.	The **Carnean festival** at Sparta founded with musical contests, at which *Terpander* was victorious. (Athenaeus, xiv. 635.) The festival occupied nine days in August.
675.	26.2.	**Chalcedon** founded by Megara. (Strabo, 320.) Cyzicus recolonised by Megara.
673.	26.4.	**Locri** in Italy, founded by the Locrians. This is the date given by Eusebius. Others put it earlier, soon after Croton, 710; Strabo, 259.
673.	27.1.	Pantaleon, king of the Pisatans (*see* 644 B.C.), who are now independent of the Eleans.
671.	27.2.	*Alcman, the lyric poet, lived at Sparta about this time.* (Bergk, *Poet. Lyr. Graec.*, vol. iii. p. 14 ff.)
670.	27.3.	**Orthagoras becomes tyrant of Sicyon.** (His son Myron gained a victory at Olympia in Ol. 33, 648 B.C., Paus. vi. 19. 2, which brings us to this date, or a little earlier for Orthagoras. Grote, pt. ii., c. 9.)

B.C.	OL.	
669.	27.4.	Defeat of the Spartans by the Argives at **Hysiae**. (Paus. ii. 24. 8.) By this victory the Argives secured possession of Cynuria, and maintained it till about Ol. 56.
668.	28.1.	**Capture of Eira and end of the Second Messenian War.**
667.		Assurbanipal (Sardanapalus), king of Assyria.
665.	28.4.	Gymnopaedia established at Sparta. *Thaletas the Cretan, who composed songs for the Spartans, may be placed at this date.*
664.	29.1.	**Acrae** founded by Syracuse. (Thuc. vi. 5.) Sea-fight between the Corinthians and the Corcyraeans. (Thuc. i. 13.)
660.	30.1.	**Selymbria** founded by Megara (Strabo, 319). **Zaleucus** gives laws to the Locrians, which are the oldest written laws known in Greece.
657.	30.4.	Foundation of **Byzantium** by the Megarians. *Lesches of Lesbos, an Epic poet, author of the "Little Iliad." (Kinkel, Frag. Epic. Graec. 36 ff.)*
656.	31.2.	Phraortes (656-634) ascends the throne of Media.
655.	31.2.	**Cypselus**, with the help of the demos, expels the oligarchy of the Bacchiadae from Corinth, and establishes himself as tyrant. (Arist. *Pol.* v. 9. 22.)
654.	31.3.	Acanthus and Stagira in Chalcidice, colonies founded by Andros. (Strabo, 7. *fr.* 31.) Abdera founded by Clazomenae, but the colony was expelled by the Thracians. (Hdt. i. 168.) Istros, Lampsacus, and Borysthenes, founded by Miletus. (Strabo, 319, 589, 305.)
650.	30.3.	**Psammetichus I.**, king of Egypt. About this time he succeeded in establishing himself with the aid of Greek and Carian mercenaries: Previously, he had been a vassal-king of the Assyrians.
648.	33.1.	Himera founded by Zancle. (Strabo, 273.) *Pisander the Epic poet, author of a poem on the labours of Heracles (Suidas). He was a native of Camirus in Rhodes (Kinkel, Frag. Epic. Graec., 248).* In this Olympiad **Myron** of Sicyon was victor in the chariot race. (Paus. vi. 19. 2.)

B.C.	OL.	
644.	34.1.	**Casmenae** founded by Syracuse. The Pisatans celebrate the Olympic games under Pantaleon their king. (According to Africanus, the Pisatans, together with the Eleans, celebrated the Olympiads from Ol. 27 to Ol. 52. But in Ol. 8 and 34 they apparently refused the Eleans any share. Cp. B.C. 748, 364.)
640.	33.1.	About this time we must place **Charondas** the lawgiver of Catana. (Diodorus, xii. 14, gives a false account of his laws, as adapted to Thurii.)
635.	36.2.	The Cimmerians take Sardis a second time. (Hdt. i. 15.)
634.	36.3.	**Cyaxares** (634-594) succeeds Phraortes in Media. (Hdt. i. 102.) The Scythians invade Asia.
631.	37.2.	**Cyrene** founded by Battus of Thera (631-591). (Hdt. iv. 154.)
630.	37.3.	**Naucratis** founded by Miletus in Egypt. (Strabo, p. 801.)
629- 617.		*Mimnermus of Colophon, the Elegiac poet.* (Bergk, *Poet. Lyr. Graec.*, ii. 25 ff.) Sadyattes, king of Lydia. (Hdt. i. 16).
628.	38.1.	**Selinus** founded by Hyblaean Megara. (Thuc. vi. 4, a hundred years after the foundation of Megara, 728 B.C.)
625.	38.4.	**Periander** succeeds Cypselus at Corinth. **Theagenes, tyrant of Megara**, father-in-law of **Cylon of Athens**. (Arist. *Pol.* v. 4, 5 ; Thuc. i. 126.) Corinth and Corcyra found Epidamnus, Ambracia, Anactorium, Leucas, and Apollonia. Periander married Melissa the daughter of **Procles, tyrant of Epidaurus** (Hdt. iii. 50), who must therefore be placed about this time. *Arion of Methymna in Lesbos, the lyric poet, is a contemporary of Periander. He introduced the "Cyclic Choruses."* (Hdt. i. 23 ; Bergk, *Poet. Lyr. Graec.*, iii. 79.) At this time **Babylon** became independent of Assyria under **Nabopolassar** (625-605).
623.	39.2.	War between Miletus and Sadyattes of Lydia. (Hdt. i. 17, 18.)

B.C.	OL.	
621.	39.4.	**Laws of Draco.** (Clem. Al., *Strom.* i. p. 309.) These laws were noted for their severity, death being nearly always the penalty imposed. (Arist. *Pol.* ii. 12.)
620.	40.1.	**Cylon attempts to establish himself as tyrant at Athens.** (Thuc. i. 126.) Cylon's victory at Olympia is placed by Africanus at Ol. 35, 640 B.C. The date of the attempt is uncertain; it took place after Draco, and before Epimenides came to Athens. Megacles was archon at this time (Plut. *Sol.* c. 12). It also took place in an Olympian year, and if this year is not accepted, 616 or 612 must be the date.
617.	40.4.	Alyattes (617-560) succeeds Sadyattes as king of Lydia. (Hdt. i. 25.)
615.	41.1.	Necho succeeds Psammetichus I. in Egypt. (Hdt. ii. 157-161.) War between Lydia and Media. It lasted five years, and came to an end owing to an eclipse in 610 B.C. (Hdt. i. 74.) (But others prefer the eclipse of 585 B.C.)
612.	42.1.	Peace between Lydia and Miletus. **Thrasybulus tyrant of Miletus.**
611.	42.2.	**Pittacus** overthrows the tyranny of Melanchrus in Mitylene with the help of the brothers of Alcaeus. (Arist. *Pol.* iii. 9. 5.)
610.	42.3.	*Alcaeus of Mitylene.* (Hdt. v. 94.) *Sappho and Erinna of Lesbos.* (Bergk, *Poet. Lyr.* iii. 82.) *Stesichorus of Himera in Sicily, author of a poem on Helen.*
606.	43.3.	**Fall of Nineveh,** which is taken by Cyaxares. The fall of Nineveh should probably be placed earlier, in 625 B.C., the dominion of the Scythians lasting but seven or eight years. (Maspero, *Histoire de l'Orient*, p. 476.)
600.	45.1.	Massilia founded by Phocaea.
599.	45.2.	Camarina founded by Syracuse. (Thuc. vi. 5, 135 years after Syracuse.) The Alcmaeonids expelled from Athens, on account of their conduct in the matter of Cylon. (Thuc. i. 126.)

B.C.	OL.	
596.	46.1.	*Epimenides* of Crete visits Athens, and purifies the city. (Plut. *Sol.* 12).
		Chilon of Sparta. (Hdt. i. 59.)
595.	46.2.	Outbreak of the **First Sacred or Cirrhaean War**, which lasted ten years. (600-590, Curtius.)
		Psammetichus II., king of Egypt (595-589.)
594.	46.3.	**Solon, archon at Athens.**
		LEGISLATION OF SOLON.
		Solon's elegies. (Bergk, vol. ii. 34 ff.)
592.	47.1.	Odessus founded by Miletus.
		Anaximander of Miletus (*Philosopher*). (Diels, p. 24. Diog. Laert., ii. 2.)
		Anacharsis, the Scythian, is said to have visited Athens about this time. (Plut. *Sol.* 5.)
591.	47.2.	In Cyrene Arcesilaus I. (591-575) succeeds Battus I. (Hdt. iv. 159.)
590.	47.3.	Crissa is taken by the Amphictyons under Eurylochus. (Strabo, 419.)
589.	47.4.	In Egypt, Psammetichus II. is succeeded by Hophrah (Apries), 589-570.
		Pittacus is "aesymnete" of Miletus. (Arist. *Pol.* iii. 14.)
588.	48.1.	**Pythagoras of Samos** is victorious in the boxing at Olympia (Diog. L., viii. 47). Damophon, son of Pantaleon, king of Pisa.
586.	48.3.	Re-institution or extension of the **Pythian games.** (Paus. x. 7. 4.)
585.	48.4.	**Periander** dies, and is succeeded by his nephew Psammetichus, the last tyrant of Corinth.
		Sacadas of Argos gained the prize for the flutes in the first three Pythiads. His songs were sung by the Messenians after their restoration, in B.C. *369.*
		(Curtius places at this date the peace between Lydia and Media. See 610 B.C. In this year also, there was an eclipse of the sun.)
582.	49.3.	**Acragas (Agrigentum)** founded by the Geloans. (Thuc. vi. 4.)
		Cleisthenes of Sicyon is victor in the second Pythiad.

B.C.	OL.	
581.	49.4.	**The tyranny in Corinth overthrown by the Spartans.**
		Psammetichus, the last tyrant, was the son of Gorgias or Gordas, and reigned three years and six months (Arist. *Pol.* v. 9). Observe that he bears the name of the Egyptian king.
579.	50.2.	**Lipara** founded by Cnidus and Rhodes. (Diod. v. 9.)
575.	51.2.	The Phocaeans attain great power by sea. Battus II. of Cyrene, succeeds Arcesilaus I.
573.	51.4.	Foundation of the (recorded) Nemean games.
572.	52.1.	**Phalaris tyrant of Agrigentum.** The Pisatans under Pyrrhus, a son of Pantaleon, are defeated by the Eleans (Paus. vi. 22. 4), and deprived of the presidency of the Olympic games.
570.	52.3.	*Aesopus (fable-poet).* (Diog. Laert. i. 72.) Amasis (570-526) dethrones Apries, king of Egypt (Hdt. ii. 169; Diod. i. 168). The Hellenion founded in Egypt at Naucratis (Hdt. ii. 170). Cyprus conquered by Egypt and made tributary (Hdt. ii. 182).
566.	53.3.	**The Panathenaea are founded at Athens.** *Eugammon of Cyrene the author of the "Telegonia."* (Kinkel, *Ep. Graec.*, p. 57 ff.)
565.	53.4.	About this time may be placed the great sea-fight between Perinthus and Megara, and the revolution at Samos. (Plut. *Quaest. Graec.* 56.)
564.	54.1.	Alalia founded by Phocaea, twenty years before the attack of Harpagus on Phocaea. (Hdt. i. 168.)
563.	54.2.	Amisus founded by Phocaea, according to Scymnus, *f.* 181 (but see Strabo, p. 547).
560.	55.1.	**Anaxandridas and Ariston, kings of Sparta.** **Peisistratus becomes tyrant of Athens for the first time.**
		Curtius gives the following dates for Peisistratus: 1st tyranny, 560-559. 2d tyranny, 554-553. At Eretria, 552-541. 3d tyranny, 541-527.

B.C.	OL.	
560.	55.1.	**Croesus** (560-546), king of Lydia, succeeds Alyattes, and makes war on the Greeks of Asia. *Pherecydes of Syros.* (*Rise of Greek prose.*) Cleisthenes of Sicyon cannot be put much later than this year, for Aristotle says that the dynasty (the Orthagoridae) lasted 100 years (*Pol.* v. 9. 21); and not much earlier, for the son of his daughter, who was married in his lifetime (Hdt. vi. 125 ff.), was Cleisthenes of Athens. (See 670, 502, 509.)
559.	55.2.	Heracleia (in Pontus) founded by Miletus. (Strabo, 541.) **Defeat of Astyages, and overthrow of the Median Empire by Cyrus.**
556.	56.1.	Chilon Ephor at Sparta. (560 according to Diog. Laertius.) The Chilon mentioned in Hdt. v. 41, vi. 25, as the father of the wife of Leotychides, must have been the grandson of the great Chilon.
554.	56.3.	Tegea acknowledges the hegemony of Sparta. (Hdt. i. 66 ff.) This must be previous to the inquiries of Croesus respecting the position of the states of Greece, with a view to alliance.
553.	56.4.	Destruction of Camarina, by Syracuse. It was afterwards recolonised by Hippocrates. (Hdt. vii. 154.)
548.	58.1.	**The temple at Delphi burnt.** (Paus. x. 5. 13.) It was rebuilt by the Alcmaeonidae (Hdt. v. 62) after they had been enriched by Croesus. (Hdt. vi. 125.)
546.	58.3.	**Capture of Sardis by Cyrus.** Overthrow of the Lydian empire; the Greeks in Asia Minor and the adjacent islands become subject to Persia. *Anaximenes of Miletus*, the philosopher, is to be placed at this date. (Diels, 27.) Duncker fixes the capture of Sardis at 549, on the ground that Croesus must have fallen before the temple at Delphi was burnt, and his offerings injured. 546 is the date given by Eusebius.
543	59.2.	The Phocaeans expelled from home by Harpagus, the general of Cyrus, found Velia in lower Italy; the Teans take refuge in Abdera. (Hdt. i. 167, 168.)

E

B.C.	OL.	
543.	59.2.	**Anacreon of Teos; Ibycus of Rhegium.** (Bergk, iii. 235 ff.) *Theognis of Megara.* (Bergk, ii. 117.) The "*floruit*" of Theognis is placed by Eusebius in 546, by Jerome in 541. Suidas says that he was born in 544. As he lived to see the battle of *Plataea* (cp. vers. 773 ff.), he cannot have been born much before 550 B.C. The date of Eusebius would therefore seem too early.
540.	60.1.	*Xenophanes "floruit."* (Diog. Laert. ix. 20.) If the ἀκμή be fixed at 40 years, the birth of Xenophanes will fall in 580. He lived on to the time of Cyrus and Darius (Apollodorus in Clem. Alex. *Strom.* p. 350; Diels, p. 22). Amyntas I., king of Macedonia.
538.	60.3.	**Capture of Babylon by Cyrus.** Overthrow of the Babylonian kingdom.
537.	60.4.	About this time or earlier (see 560 B.C.), **Peisistratus becomes tyrant of Athens for the third time.** The tyranny is now continuous to the expulsion of Hippias, in 510 B.C.
535.	61.2.	*Thespis of Icaria, the founder of Attic tragedy.*
532.	62.1.	**Polycrates, tyrant of Samos.** (Hdt. iii. 39-46, etc.) *Phocylides of Miletus, author of elegiac and gnomic poems* (Bergk, ii. 98). *Hipponax of Ephesus* (Bergk, ii. 460). *Pythagoras is now about 40 years old* (Diels, p. 25).
529.	62.4.	**Death of Cyrus;** Cambyses succeeds (529-521). Period of the greatest extent of the Samian empire.
527.	63.2.	**Death of Peisistratus;** his son Hippias succeeds him. Of the 33 years from 560, he had been tyrant 17. (Arist. *Pol.* v. 12.)
526.	63.3.	Amasis of Egypt is succeeded by his son Psammenitus (Psammetichus III.).
525.	63.4.	**Cambyses conquers Egypt.** The Lacedaemonians attack Polycrates. (Hdt. iii. 39, 44.)
524.	64.1.	Miltiades, archon at Athens.

B.C.	OL.	
522.	64.3.	**Polycrates of Samos** is put to death by Oroetes about this time.
521.	64.4.	Death of **Cambyses, king of Persia**; Pseudo-Smerdis usurps for seven months; Darius, son of Hystaspes, recovers the kingdom for the Persians (521-485).
520.	65.1.	**Cleomenes, king of Sparta.** His attack on Argolis.
		Pausanias puts the attack on Argolis immediately after the accession of Cleomenes, but as it is closely connected with the fall of Miletus in 494 (Hdt. vi. 77), and as Herodotus tells of the Argives, in 481 (vii. 149) B.C., that Cleomenes had recently slain 6000 citizens, the invasion should be placed later (495 B.C. Duncker). Cleomenes is king of Sparta when Maeandrius arrives from Samos (Hdt. iii. 148), *i.e.* in 516 (Duncker), but Dorieus leaves Lacedaemon soon after his accession (see 510 B.C.).
519.	65.2.	**Plataea seeks the protection of Athens** in the 93d year before 427 (Thuc. iii. 68). Cp. Hdt. vi. 108.
515.	66.2.	Expedition of Darius against the Scythians. Miltiades III. is tyrant of the Chersonese at this time.
514.	66.3.	Campaign of Megabazus in Thrace and Macedonia. Murder of Hipparchus, at the time of the great Panathenaea. (Hdt. v. 55; Thuc. vi. 56-58.)
510.	67.3.	**Cleomenes and Demaratus, kings of Sparta.** **Hippias expelled** (Hdt. v. 65) by Cleomenes and the Spartans. **Destruction of Sybaris by Croton**; Dorieus of Lacedaemon. (Hdt. v. 43-45.) Amyntas, king of Macedonia, offers Anthemus to Hippias. (Hdt. v. 94.) Cp. 540 B.C.
509.	67.4.	**The Constitution of Cleisthenes. The four Tribes increased to ten, and the Demes divided among them. The senate made up to 500.**
508.	68.1.	Isagoras, archon at Athens; Cleisthenes expelled from Athens with the help of Cleomenes of Sparta, but recalled after a short time.

B.C.	OL.	
507.	68.2.	**March of the Peloponnesians under Cleomenes and Demaratus, to establish Isagoras at Athens.** The Peloponnesian army is disbanded, owing to the dissension of its leaders, and the opposition of the Corinthians; the Thebans and Chalcidians attack the Athenians, but are defeated; **first instance of Athenian Cleruchi at Chalcis.** (Hdt. v. 74 ff.)
		The Aeginetans join the Thebans against Athens, and attack Attica without proclamation of war (Hdt. v. 81). A subsequent attempt was made at Sparta to restore Hippias, but owing to the opposition of Corinth, the allies refused to join in it. **Hippias repairs to Sardis and creates ill feeling against the Athenians who are bidden to take him back.** (Hdt. v. 90 ff.)
504.	69.1.	*The philosophers Heracleitus of Ephesus, Parmenides of Elea.* Heracleitus (Diels, p. 33) is placed here by Diog. ix. 1. Apparently all that is really known about him is that he lived in the time of Darius. Apollodorus placed Xenophanes in Ol. 79 (Diog. ix. 29), and Parmenides in Ol. 69 (Diog. ix. 23). Plato, *Parm.* 127 ff., represents Zeno as 25 years younger than Parmenides. (Diels, p. 34.)
501.	69.4.	**The attempt of Aristagoras upon Naxos.** (Hdt. v. 30 ff.) Naxos at this time was in great prosperity, and able to put 8000 men in the field, besides possessing ships of war. Oligarchical exiles from the island apply to Aristagoras, who is now governor of Miletus in the place of Histiaeus. He undertakes to restore them, with the help of Persia. Two hundred triremes are put at his disposal by Artaphernes, satrap of Sardis, but owing to a quarrel with Megabates, the commander, news is sent to Naxos of the approach of the fleet. After a delay of four months, the siege is abandoned. The fleet set out in the spring. (Hdt. v. 34, *ib.* 31.)
500.	70.1.	**Aristagoras,** in despair at his failure, and encouraged by Histiaeus, who wishes to return from Susa, revolts. He lays down his tyranny, and in the Ionian cities establishes strategi in the place of tyrants (Hdt. v. 37). Then he **proceeds to Sparta in order to solicit help**;

B.C.	OL.	
500.	70.1.	unable to move Cleomenes, he is more successful at Athens. (Hdt. v. 50 ff., 97.)
		Hecataeus of Miletus the logographer, urged the Ionian cities not to share in the revolt. (Hdt. v. 36.)
499.	70.2.	**REVOLT OF THE IONIANS FROM PERSIA. 499-493.**
		The Ionians, aided by troops from Athens and Eretria, surprise Sardis and burn it; they are defeated on their return to Ephesus. (Hdt. v. 99 ff.)
		The towns on the Hellespont, in Caria, and the island of Cyprus, join the revolt.
498.	70.3.	**Second year of the Ionian revolt.**
		Cyprus reconquered by the Persians; after a year of freedom. (Hdt. v. 116.)
		The towns in the Hellespont reconquered. War in Caria. (Hdt. v. 117, 118.)
497.	70.4.	**Third year of the Ionian revolt.**
		Aristagoras retires to Myrcinus, and is slain while besieging a Thracian town. (Hdt. v. 126.)
496.	71.1.	**Fourth year of the Ionian revolt.** Histiaeus is permitted to return from Susa to the coast. (Hdt. vi. 1.)
495.	71.2.	**Fifth year of the Ionian revolt.** Histiaeus fails to excite a rebellion at Sardis, and retires to the Hellespont. (Hdt. vi. 4 ff.)
		Birth of Sophocles the poet.
494.	71.3.	**Sixth year of the Ionian revolt.**
		The Ionian fleet defeated at Lade and Miletus conquered. (Hdt. vi. 18.)
		Aeaces is restored to Samos by the Persians.
		Samian exiles at Zancle in Sicily.
		Histiaeus at Chios. His capture and execution by Artaphernes.
493.	71.4.	Chios, Lesbos, and Tenedos, reduced by the Persian fleet. Other islands conquered. **The revolt entirely suppressed.**
		Themistocles, archon at Athens.
		Miltiades retires from the Chersonese to Athens. (Hdt. vi. 41.)

B.C.	OL.	
493.	71.4.	Hippocrates, tyrant of Gela.
		Anaxilaus of Rhegium.
492.	72.1.	**The first expedition of the Persians against Greece** under Mardonius sets out in the spring. (Hdt. vi. 43.)
		The fleet is almost totally destroyed off Mt. Athos, and the army in Thrace. (Hdt. vi. 45.)
491.	72.2.	Darius sends heralds to the Greeks to demand earth and water.
		War of Athens and Aegina. 491-481. (Hdt. vi. 89.)
		New preparations of Darius.
		Demaratus of Sparta is deposed, Cleomenes dies.
		Leotychides and Leonidas, kings of Sparta.
		Gelon becomes tyrant of Gela.
		Phrynichus, the tragic poet, produced his play of the "Capture of Miletus" about this time.
490.	72.3.	**FIRST PERSIAN WAR. The Persians under Datis and Artaphernes (with Hippias) sail across the Aegean Sea, land on Euboea, take Eretria, and then land on the plain of Marathon, where they are defeated by the Athenians and Plataeans, under the command of Miltiades, on the 6th of Boedromion.** (Hdt. vi. ; Plut. *Camil.* c. 19.)
		Earthquake at Delos.
		Aeschylus present at the battle of Marathon.
489.	72.4.	Aristeides, archon at Athens.
		Miltiades attacks Paros and fails: his condemnation and death.
		Panyasis, an Epic poet, uncle of Herodotus, about this time. He wrote a "Heracleis." (Kinkel, *Frag. Epic. Graec.*, p. 253.)
		Theron, tyrant of Agrigentum.
487.	73.2.	*Chionides, the comic poet, began to exhibit, according to Suidas.*
486.	73.3.	**Egypt revolts from Persia**: this delays the threatened invasion of Greece. (Hdt. vii. 1. 4.)
485.	73.4.	**Xerxes becomes king of Persia in the room of Darius.**

B.C.	OL.	
485.	73.4.	Gelo, master of Syracuse. *Epicharmus, the comedian, still exhibits in Syracuse.* Death of Darius, accession of Xerxes (485-465).
484.	74.1.	**Egypt is recovered by the Persians.** *About this time may be placed the birth of Herodotus.*
483.	74.2.	**Aristeides ostracised.**
482.	74.3.	**Themistocles, archon at Athens.** Themistocles lays the foundation of the maritime power of Athens, by persuading the Athenians to expend the revenues from the silver mines at Laurium on the building of triremes, and to construct the harbour of Peiraeus (Hdt. vii. 143). The war between Athens and Aegina is still raging, and the triremes were built primarily for this.
481.	74.4.	**Xerxes passes the winter at Sardis to be ready for his campaign in the spring.** (Hdt. vii. 32 ff.) The Greeks assemble at the Isthmus; and send to Gelon for help. (Hdt. vii. 145 ff., 156.)
480.	75.1.	Calliades archon at Athens. **SECOND PERSIAN WAR. Xerxes sets out in the spring against Greece at the head of a fleet and an army. The Spartan king, Leonidas, takes up his position with 300 Spartans and other troops from the rest of Greece in the pass of Thermopylae. He is overpowered. The Greek fleet fights two engagements with the Persian at Artemisium, and retires, on hearing the news of the loss of Thermopylae, to Salamis.** Pleistarchus succeeds Leonidas as king of Sparta. His guardians are Cleombrotus and afterwards Pausanias. **The battle of Salamis on the 20th of Boedromion. Xerxes flees, leaving 300,000 men in Greece under the command of Mardonius. Athens occupied by the Persians.** *The Lyric poets, Simonides, Pindar, Bacchylides.* (Bergk, i. ii. 380, 569.) *The tragic poet Aeschylus.*

B.C.	OL.	
480.	75.1.	Thero and Gelo defeat the Carthaginians at Himera. (Hdt. vii. 166.)
479.	75.1.	Xanthippus archon at Athens. On the 4th of Boedromion occurred the victory of the Hellenes at Plataea, under Pausanias and Aristeides, who has been recalled from banishment, by which an end was made of the Persian invasion. Victory of the Greek fleet at Mycale. The Greeks determine to pursue the war and liberate the Asiatic Greeks. Siege of Sestos. *The "History" of Herodotus closes at this point.*
478.	75.3.	Athens is rebuilt and surrounded with a wall, by the energy of Themistocles. Hiero succeeds Gelo as tyrant of Syracuse.
477.	75.4.	The harbour of Peiraeus is now completed and surrounded with a wall. The constitution is made more democratic by the action of Aristeides, who proposes that the 4th Solonian class should be capable of holding office. The Hellenic fleet, under the command of Pausanias, carries on the war against Persia.
476.	76.1.	Conquest of Cyprus by Pausanias. (Thuc. i. 94, 98.) Conquest of Byzantium. (Thuc. *ib.*) Treachery of Pausanias. The command of the Greek fleet is transferred to Athens. Beginning of the Athenian Empire. Hiero, tyrant of Syracuse and Gela. His court becomes the home of many distinguished Greeks: Aeschylus, Pindar, Simonides. (Diod. xi. 51 ff.)
475.	76.2.	Organisation of the Confederacy of Delos. (Thuc. i. 96.) The revenue fixed at 460 talents.
474.	76.3.	Hiero defeats the Tuscans. (Diod. xi. 51.)
472.	77.1.	*The "Persae" of Aeschylus in the spring of this year* (in the archonship of Menon). (*Arg. Pers.*)

B.C.	OL.	
472.	77.1.	Death of Thero, tyrant of Agrigentum. Thrasydaeus, his son, is defeated by Hiero. (Diod. xi. 53.)
471.	77.2.	**Themistocles ostracised.** He goes to Argos. (Thuc. i. 135.) Cimon becomes the leader of the Greeks, and conquers Eion and Scyrus. (Thuc. i. 98.) *Timocreon of Rhodes, a lyric poet, wrote against Thucydides, the son of Melesias.*
470.	77.3.	Carystus conquered by the Athenians. (Thuc. i. 98.)
469.	77.4.	Leotychides is banished; Archidamus, king of Sparta.
468.	78.1.	*Sophocles obtains a victory over Aeschylus.* (Plut. *Cim.* c. 8.) **Death of Aristeides** (Plut. *Arist.* c. 26); beginning of the influence of Pericles. **Mycenae is destroyed by the Argives.** (Diod. xi. 65.)
467.	78.2.	**Death of Hiero, tyrant of Syracuse.** (Diod. xi. 66.) He is followed by Thrasybulus, his brother. In Rhegium and Zancle Micythus resigns the power into the hands of the sons of Anaxilaus. (Diod. *ib.*)
466.	78.3.	**Naxos refuses her contingent to the alliance, and is reduced by the Athenians.** (Thuc. i. 98.) **Double victory of Cimon over the Persians at Eurymedon.** Themistocles passes over from Argos to Persia, where, after a time, he dies. (Thuc. i. 137.) End of the Tyranny, and establishment of Democracy at Syracuse. (Diod. xi. 67, 68.)
465.		At this time the Athenians attempt to found a colony at **Amphipolis**; 10,000 colonists slain by the Thracians at Drabescus. (Thuc. iv. 102.) **Death of Xerxes** (Diod. xi. 69). He was assassinated by Artabanus; Artaxerxes succeeds (465-425).

B.C.	OL.	
464.	79.1.	**Earthquake at Sparta, and revolt of the Helots.** (Thuc. i. 101.) Cimon marches to the aid of the Lacedaemonians. (Thuc. i. 102; Plut. *Cim.* c. 16.) This is sometimes called the third Messenian war.
463.	79.2.	**Thasos reduced by Athens.** (Thuc. i. 101.) *Xanthus, the Lydian, wrote history in the time of Artaxerxes.* (Strabo, 49.)
461.	79.4.	**The Athenians**, offended by the conduct of the Spartans before Ithome, **banish Cimon**, who seems to have gone a second time to their aid, **renounce the alliance with Sparta, and conclude an alliance with Argos**, which is joined by Thessaly and Megara, who are at war with Corinth. (Thuc. i. 102, 103.) **Building of the Long Walls of Megara.** (Thuc. *ib.*)
460.	80.1.	About this time **Pericles and Ephialtes lessen the power of Areopagus. Introduction of pay for the jurors.** The Athenians send an expedition to Egypt for the support of Inarus, who had revolted against the Persian king. (Thuc. i. 104.) *Birth of Democritus* (Diels, p. 30). *He wrote his* Μικρὸς Διάκοσμος *730 years after the taking of Troy. If we assume that he wrote it when 40 years old, his date for Troy is* 1150.
459.	80.2.	Cimon is ostracised.
458.	80.3.	*The "Oresteia" of Aeschylus acted in the spring of this year.* (*Arg. Agam.*)
	?	**The Athenians at war with Corinth, Epidaurus and Aegina.** On land they are victorious at Halieis, and by sea at Cecryphaleia. They gain a second victory, still more decisive, at Aegina; Aegina besieged. (Thuc. i. 105.) The Corinthians invade the Megarid in order to relieve Aegina, but are defeated by Myronides at the head of the youngest and oldest of the Athenian citizens. (Thuc. i. 107, 108.) About this time the Athenians take Naupactus from the Ozolian Locrians. (Thuc. i. 103.)

B.C.	OL.	
457.	80.4.	**Cimon recalled.** (Thuc. i. 108.) **Battle of Tanagra, in which the Spartans at the head of a Peloponnesian army defeat the Athenians.** (Thuc. i. 108.)
456.	81.1.	**The Athenians under Myronides conquer the Boeotians at Oenophyta**; whereupon Boeotia, Phocis, and Opuntian Locris join the Athenian alliance. **Completion of the long walls from Athens to the Peiraeus and Phalerum. Aegina reduced to subjection.** (Thuc. i. 108.) *Death of Aeschylus.*
455.	81.2.	The Athenians under the command of Tolmides sail round Peloponnesus. (Thuc. i. 108.) The third Messenian war ended by the capture of Ithome; the Athenians give Naupactus to the Messenians. **The Athenian army and fleet in Egypt are annihilated** (Thuc. i. 110). Amyrtaeus still maintains himself in the marshes. (Hdt. ii. 140; Thuc. i. 110.)
454.	81.3.	Pericles in the Crissaean Gulf. (Thuc. i. 111.) Achaia joins the Athenian alliance. About this time may be placed the removal of the Chest of the Confederacy of Delos to Athens, as the tribute lists date from this year.
450.	82.3.	**Five years' truce between Athens and Sparta.** (Thuc. i. 112.) Thirty years' peace between Sparta and Argos. *The tragic poets, Sophocles, Euripides.* *Ion of Chios.* *Anaxagoras the philosopher withdraws from Athens.*
449.	82.4.	**The Athenians resume the war against Persia** under Cimon, and **after Cimon's death win a double victory at Salamis in Cyprus** over the Phoenicians, Cyprians, and Cilicians. (Thuc. i. 112.) *The comic poets Crates, Cratinus.*
448.	83.1.	**Attack of the Phocians on Delphi, which leads to new hostilities between Athens and Sparta.**

B.C.	OL.	
448.	83.1.	The philosophers Zeno and Anaxagoras. Anaxagoras (Diels, 28) was born, according to Apollodorus, in Ol. 70.1. (=500) and died in 88.1.=428. (Diog. Laert. ii. 7.)
447.	83.2.	**Battle of Coronea.** The Athenians evacuate Boeotia. (Thuc. i. 113.) Defeat of the Sybarites by the Crotoniates. (Diod. xii. 9 ff.)
445.	83.4.	**Euboea and Megara** revolt from the Athenian alliance; the Peloponnesians, under the Spartan king Pleistoanax, invade Attica, but retire without inflicting any damage upon the Athenians. Euboea reconquered by Pericles (Thuc. i. 114), and the Hestiaean territory allotted to Cleruchi. **Thirty years' peace between Athens and Sparta.** (Thuc. i. 115.) Athens abandons the empire by land. *Pheidias, Polycleitus, Myron, sculptors. Polygnotus the painter.*

YEARS OF PEACE BETWEEN ATHENS AND SPARTA. 445-431.

444.	84.1.	The Athenian citizens are subjected to a scrutiny and a large number are struck off the roll. The occasion of the scrutiny was a gift of corn from Egypt. (Schol. to Aristoph. *Vesp.* 716.) Pericles in sole possession of the government at Athens. **Another wall is built from Athens to the Peiraeus. Date of the Cimonian peace. Callias in Susa.** (Hdt. vii. 151.)
443.	84.2.	Thurii founded by the Athenians. (Diod. xii. 11.) *Empedocles floruit.* (Diels, p. 37 ; Diog. viii. 52.) He died in 424. Among the colonists who went to Thurii were *Herodotus the historian, and Lysias the orator,* who at this time was fifteen years old. *Hippodamus of Miletus, the architect.* (Arist. *Pol.* ii. 8.)

[440-432.]   81

B.C.	OL.	
440.	85.1.	**Samos and Miletus at war about Priene. The Milesians apply to Athens.** (Thuc. i. 115; Diod. xii. 27, 28.)
		Samos was besieged for nine months. Sophocles was one of the generals in the war, elected, it is said, in consequence of the success of his *Antigone*, which is therefore placed in 441 or 440. (*Ant. Argt.*)
		Comedies prohibited for this year and the two next. (Schol. *Acharn.* 67.)
439.	85.2.	Samos conquered.
438.	85.3.	**The Parthenon at Athens completed.** *The "Alcestis" of Euripides.* (*Argt. Alc.*)
437.	85.4.	**A colony sent to Amphipolis under Agnon.** (Diod. xii. 32.)
436.	86.1.	In this year the building of the Propylaea at Athens was commenced. *Cratinus the comic poet. Pheidias* at Olympia.
435.	86.2.	**Battle at sea between the Corcyreans and Corinthians at Actium.** The Corcyreans completely victorious, and compel Epidamnus to capitulate. (Thuc. i. 29.)
434.	86.3.	Naval preparations on the part of Corcyra and Corinth, in consequence of the late battle. (Thuc. i. 31.)
433.	86.4.	**Corcyrean and Corinthian embassies to Athens. Athens forms a defensive alliance with Corcyra.** The Propylaea completed (437-433).
432.	87.1.	In the spring, the naval engagements at **Sybota** take place, and in the summer **Potidaea**, a colony of Corinth, revolts from the Athenian alliance. It is reduced to a state of siege. **Congress at Sparta.** The war resolved upon. Pericles advises the Athenians to resist the Spartan demands, and excludes the Megarians from the market of Athens. (Thuc. bk. i.)
		About this time Anaxagoras, who had returned

B.C.	OL.	
431.	87.1.	to Athens, Aspasia and Pheidias are persecuted by the opponents of Pericles. Death of Pheidias.
		Meton arranges a new cycle of nineteen years, and publishes a calendar.
		THE PELOPONNESIAN WAR. 431-404. *First year of the War.* (Thuc. ii. 1-47.)
		Spring. **Attack of the Thebans on Plataea, under the command of two Boeotarchs, Pythangelus and Diemporus.** The Plataeans maintain the city when the first surprise is over, capture the Thebans, and put their prisoners to death (Thuc. ii. 2-6), including Eurymachus, who planned the whole. General preparations for war, the feeling being strongly against the Athenians. The Lacedaemonian allies summoned at the Isthmus, in order to invade Attica.
		The Athenians collect at Athens. Their discomfort.
	87.2.	*Summer.* **First invasion of Attica** (80 days after the attack on Plataea, in the middle of the summer), under Archidamus (they ravage Oenoe, Eleusis, the Thriasian plain, and Acharnae, returning by Oropus).
		A fleet of 100 Attic ships, with 50 Corcyrean, cruises round Peloponnesus. Attack on Methone, which is saved by Brasidas; they ravage Pheia, take Sollium, Astacus, and Cephallenia, and return home.
		The Athenians set aside 1000 talents, and 100 of the best ships each year, to form a reserve.
		Expulsion of the Aeginetans; part of whom are settled in Thyrea.
		Eclipse of the sun.
		The Athenians form an alliance with Sitalces, and come to terms with Perdiccas.
		End of Summer. Megara invaded by Pericles and the entire Athenian force. This invasion repeated every year till the capture of Nisaea.

B.C.	OL.	
431.	87.1.	*Winter.* Evarchus restored to Astacus by the Corinthians.
		The Athenians celebrate the funeral of the dead.
		The *"Medea"* of Euripides. (*Argt. Med.*)
430.		*Second year of the War.* (Thuc. ii. 47-70.)
		Summer. **Second invasion of Attica by the Peloponnesians, penetrating as far as Laurium.** They remained 40 days, the longest stay which they ever made.
		Plague of Athens.
	87.3.	The Athenians sail round Peloponnesus with 100 ships under Pericles, and 50 from Lesbos and Chios; Epidaurus, Troezen, and Hermione ravaged; Prasiae destroyed.
		The fleet then sails to Potidaea under Hagnon, but soon returns, owing to the plague.
		Pericles is fined, but he soon regains the popular favour.
		Lacedaemonian ambassadors on their way to Persia are detained by Sitalces and given up to the Athenians, who convey them to Athens, and put them to death.
		The Ambraciots expel the Amphilochian Argives from their city, but are in turn expelled by the Argives, Acarnanians, and Athenians. Alliance of the Acarnanians and Athens.
		Winter. **Phormio at Naupactus.**
		The Potidaeans capitulate. They are allowed to leave the city on terms, but the Athenians are dissatisfied with their generals.
		Hermippus, the comic poet.
429.		*Third year of the War.* (Thuc. ii. 70-end.)
		Summer. Instead of invading Attica, the Lacedaemonians proceed to Plataea.
	87.4.	**Siege of Plataea.**
		The Athenians in Chalcidice. Their operations ineffective.
		The Lacedaemonians assist the Ambraciots and Chaonians against Acarnania. Failure of the

B.C.	OL.	
429.	87.4.	attack on Stratus. The Lacedaemonians return home.
		Phormio defeats the Peloponnesians in the Corinthian gulf. Brasidas and others sent to advise the Spartan commander Cnemus. Second victory of the Athenians.
		Winter. The Peloponnesians make an abortive attack on Peiraeus. They ravage Salamis and retire.
		Sitalces and the Athenians attack Perdiccas. After a time he is persuaded by Seuthes, his nephew, to return home.
		The Athenians under Phormio make an expedition into Acarnania and return to Naupactus.
428.		*Fourth year of the War.* (Thuc. iii. 1-25.)
		Spring. Phormio returns to Athens with his captives, etc.
		Summer. **Third invasion of Attica.**
		Revolt of Lesbos. Mitylene blockaded, the Mityleneans send ambassadors to Olympia.
	88.1.	The Athenians again ravage the coast of Laconia. Defeat and death of Asopus at Leucas.
		A project of attacking Attica by sea is given up by the Peloponnesians: great extent of the Athenian navy at this time.
		The Peloponnesians, though they make alliance with Mitylene, delay assistance.
		Paches blockades the city by land.
		Winter. A property tax levied for the first time at Athens.
		The Plataeans attempt to break out and succeed in part.
		The "Hippolytus" of Euripides.
427.		*Fifth year of the War.* (Thuc. iii. 25-89.)
		Spring. Salaethus sent from Lacedaemon to Mitylene to announce the help that is coming.
		Summer. The Peloponnesians send 42 ships to Mitylene under Alcidas.

B.C.	OL.	
427.	88.2.	**Fourth invasion of Attica, which caused greater distress than any except the second.**
		Mitylene capitulates. (Salaethus had armed the common people, who at once turned upon the nobles.)
		The Athenians meet to decide on the fate of the city. Cleon proposes to put all to death. Diodotus wishes milder measures. Vacillation of the Athenians, who first decide for Cleon, and send out Paches, then for Diodotus, and countermand their orders. Alcidas the Spartan admiral in the Aegean. On the approach of Paches, he returns to Peloponnesus.
		Paches at Notium. He prepares to carry out the proposals of Cleon, but is prevented by the arrival of fresh orders.
		Narrow escape of the Mityleneans. **Division of the lands of Lesbos among the Athenians.**
		Minoa captured and fortified by Nicias.
		Surrender of Plataea; the inhabitants put to death; the city razed to the ground.
		Alcidas and Brasidas sail to Corcyra. **The Corcyrean sedition suspended by the presence of Athenians and Peloponnesians.**
		War in Italy between Syracuse and Leontini. The Athenians assist the latter.
		Winter. The plague re-appears.
		The Athenians make a fruitless attack on the Aeolian islands.
		The *"Banqueters" of Aristophanes*.
426.		*Sixth year of the War.* (Thuc. iii. 89-end.)
		Summer. **No invasion of Attica owing to the earthquakes.**
	88.3.	The Athenians in Sicily; Laches captures Myle.
		Demosthenes sent with a fleet round Peloponnesus; Nicias goes to Melos; and afterwards to Tanagra, which is attacked with the whole Athenian force.
		The Lacedaemonians found Heraclea.
		Demosthenes attacks Leucas, but is persuaded to

B.C.	OL.	
426.	88.3.	make war on the Aetolians. He is repulsed, and retires to Naupactus. **The Spartans aid the Aetolians; their commander, Eurylochus, marches to their assistance through Locris, against Naupactus.**
		Winter. Delos purified; Delian games restored. **The Spartans and Ambraciots resolve to attack Amphilochian Argos: the Athenians and Acarnanians protect it.** Battles of Olpae and Idomene. **Complete defeat of the Spartans and Ambraciots.** Demosthenes returns to Athens. The Athenians resolve to send increased forces to Sicily. *The "Babylonians" of Aristophanes.*
425.		*Seventh year of the War.* (Thuc. iv. 1-52.) *Spring.* Eruption of Etna. End of the sixth year. *Summer.* Messene revolts from the Athenians. **Fifth invasion of Attica, under Agis. Ships sent to Sicily, Demosthenes with them; he wishes to fortify Pylus, and owing to stress of weather this is done.**
	88.4.	The Lacedaemonians attempt to recover it, returning from Attica for the purpose. Brasidas leads the attack, which fails. All the Spartans in the island of Sphacteria are cut off. The Spartans propose peace, but the Athenians refuse reasonable terms. Defeat of the Syracusans in the straits of Messene. The Athenians take no part in the affairs of Sicily for a time. **Blockade of Pylus.** Dissatisfaction of the Athenians. **Cleon blames the generals, and is sent out in the place of Nicias. He takes Demosthenes for his colleague.** **The island is attacked, the Lacedaemonians surrender.** Pylus garrisoned by Messenians of Naupactus. The Athenians attack the Corinthians. Battle of Solygea. They cut off Methone.

B.C.	OL.	
425.	88.4.	**The Athenians, on their way to Sicily, stop at Corcyra. Massacre of the Oligarchs owing to treachery. End of the Corcyrean sedition.**
		Winter. Anactorium occupied by the Acarnanians.
		Artaphernes, a Persian envoy, is captured on his way to Sparta from the king, at Eion. He is brought to Athens and sent to Ephesus with an Athenian embassy, but Artaxerxes was just dead, and the embassy returned.
		The Chians compelled by Athens to dismantle their walls.
		The "Acharnians" of Aristophanes.
		Death of Artaxerxes; he is succeeded by Darius II. (Nothus), 425-405.
424.	89.1.	*Eighth year of the War.* (Thuc. iv. 52-116.)
		Summer. An eclipse of the sun.
		The Lesbian refugees take Rhoeteum and Antandrus.
		The Athenians under Nicias capture Cythera.
		The Athenians attack and capture Thyrea, putting to death the Aeginetans there.
		Conference of the Sicilian states at Gela. Hermocrates of Syracuse. Peace concluded among the cities. The Athenians retire.
		Dissension at Megara; some wish to restore the exiles, some to invite the Athenians. Megara is saved, but Nisaea falls into the hands of the Athenians. Brasidas admitted at Megara by the oligarchical party, who massacre their opponents. Lasting oligarchy in Megara.
		Antandrus taken by the Athenians.
		Organisation of an invasion of Boeotia.
		Brasidas makes his way through Thessaly to Perdiccas. He is admitted into Acanthus, which revolts from Athens.
		Winter. The plot for the invasion of Boeotia is discovered. **The Athenians defeated at Delium.**
		Brasidas takes Amphipolis; banishment of Thucydides. Torone taken by Brasidas. The Megarians recover their long walls and destroy them.

B.C.	OL.	
424.	89.1.	*Spring.* **Truce for a year between Athens and Sparta.** *The "Knights" of Aristophanes.*
423.		*Ninth year of the War.* (Thuc. iv. 117—end.) *Summer.* Brasidas captures Scione, and refuses to give it up when informed of the peace. He also receives Mende, and is engaged with the Illyrians.
	89.2.	Mende recovered by the Athenians, and Scione invested. Perdiccas joins the Athenians. Thebes dismantles the walls of the Thespians. The temple of Here at Argos burnt. *Winter.* Brasidas attempts Potidaea and fails. *The "Clouds" of Aristophanes.*
422.		*Tenth year of the War.* (Thuc. v. 1-24.) *Summer.* The truce continued to the Pythian games. Second purification of Delos; removal of the inhabitants who are settled at Adramyttium. Cleon sails to Chalcidice and recaptures Torone.
	89.3.	Panactum betrayed to the Boeotians. Revolution at Leontini. The oligarchs drive out the common people and go to Syracuse, but afterwards join the commons and make war on Syracuse. Phaeax sent to Sicily. Treaty between the Locrians and Athenians. **Cleon attempts to recover Amphipolis. He fails and is slain. Brasidas also falls. The Lacedaemonian reinforcements not allowed to pass through Thessaly.** *Winter.* **Negotiations for peace; both parties to give up what they had captured, the Thebans retaining Plataea, the Athenians Nisaea.** *The "Wasps" of Aristophanes.*
421.		*Spring.* **The treaty is ratified after the city Dionysia.** Dissatisfaction of the allies, who refuse the terms. **The Lacedaemonians conclude an alliance for 50 years with Athens.** The prisoners from

B.C.	OL.	
421.	89.3.	Sphacteria are restored by the Athenians to Lacedaemon.
		Eleventh year of the War. (Thuc. v. 25-40.)
		Summer. The Corinthians urge the Argives to take the lead in the Peloponnesian confederacy. The Mantineans join the Argives, also the Eleans, Corinthians and Chalcidians.
	89.4.	The Athenians retake Scione, and after massacring the grown-up men, give the place to the Plataeans.
		Amphipolis is retained by Lacedaemon, Pylus by Athens.
		Winter. Negotiations between Boeotia and Lacedaemon. Alliance of the Boeotians and Lacedaemonians.
		Eupolis, the comic poet, exhibits his "Maricas" and "Flatterers."
		The "Peace" of Aristophanes.
		Protagoras, born 482 B.C., *died* 411 B.C. (Diels, p. 41 ; Diog. Laert. ix. 56.)
420.		*Twelfth year of the War.* (Thuc. v. 41-52.)
		Spring. Panactum destroyed. Irritation at Athens against the Lacedaemonians, which is fostered by Alcibiades.
	90.1.	Alliance between Athens and the Argive confederacy (except the Corinthians).
		The Lacedaemonians excluded from the Olympic festival.
		Winter. Defeat of the Heracleans by the neighbouring tribes.
		The "Suppliants" of Euripides.
419.	90.2.	*Thirteenth year of the War.* (Thuc. v. 55-56.)
		The Boeotians take possession of Heraclea, the Lacedaemonian colony, under the pretext of defending it against the Thessalians.
		War between Epidaurus and Argos.
		Hippias of Elis, Prodicus and Gorgias, the Sophists, Socrates.
418.	90.3.	*Fourteenth year of the War.* (Thuc. v. 57-81.)
		The Lacedaemonians aid the Epidaurians.

B.C.	OL.	
418.	90.3.	Invasion of Argolis. A truce concluded, but violated by the siege of Orchomenus by the Argives and their allies.
The Argives attack Tegea. Agis and the Lacedaemonians march out against them.
Battle of Mantinea (before the Carnean festival).
Peace between Argos and Lacedaemon.
The Argive confederacy is broken up and the democracy is put down.
417.	90.4.	*Fifteenth year of the War.* (Thuc. v. 82-83.)
The popular party at Argos attack and defeat the oligarchy, at the time of the Lacedaemonian Gymnopaediae. Renewal of the alliance with Athens. An attempt to build walls to the sea prevented by the Lacedaemonians.
The Athenians blockade Perdiccas.
Banishment of Hyperbolus.
416.	91.1.	*Sixteenth year of the War.* (Thuc. v. 84-vi. 7.)
Expedition of the Athenians against Melos. In the winter the Athenians take Melos and put the inhabitants to death.
Quarrel between Egesta and Selinus. Embassy to Athens.
Agathon, the tragic poet, wins the prize at the Lenea.
The Athenians resolve to send a large expedition to Sicily.
415.	91.2.	*Seventeenth year of the War.* (Thuc. vi. 8-93.)
The affair of the Hermae.
Attack on Alcibiades for offences against the mysteries.
The Athenians sail with a fleet of 134 ships to Sicily under Nicias, Alcibiades, and Lamachus.
Various plans of the commanders. Alcibiades recalled. The Athenians winter at Naxos. Hermocrates of Syracuse; embassies sent to Peloponnesus and Carthage. Alcibiades at Argos and Sparta.
414.	91.3.	*Eighteenth year of the War.* (Thuc. vi. 94-vii. 18.)
Gylippus the Spartan sent to Syracuse. The

B.C.	OL.	
414.	91.3.	Athenians capture Epipolae, and commence the siege of Syracuse. Death of Lamachus. **Gylippus arrives, defeats the Athenians, and prevents the city from being shut up.** The Athenians under Pythodorus make attacks on Laconia, and in connection with Perdiccas attack Amphipolis. Nicias applies for reinforcements. *The " Birds" of Aristophanes.*
413.		*Nineteenth year of the War.* (Thuc. vii. 19—viii. 6.) **The Lacedaemonians declare war on Athens.** **Deceleia in Attica occupied by the Spartans.**
	91.4.	**Demosthenes arrives with a fleet of 73 ships before Syracuse. He fails in an attack on Epipolae; the fleet is defeated in the harbour and blockaded. After a second defeat, the army retreats into the interior. Demosthenes and Nicias capitulate, and are executed, 7000 prisoners taken.** *The Gigantomachia of Hegemon* was being represented when the bad news was brought from Sicily. Archelaus, king of Macedonia (Thuc. ii. 100), surpasses all the eight kings before him in his military power. **Changes in the administration of affairs at Athens with a view to economy and defence.** *Winter.* Agis makes excursions from Deceleia. The Lacedaemonians and their allies determine to build a fleet of 100 ships. The Athenians also build ships and fortify Sunium.
412.		*Twentieth year of the War.* (Thuc. viii. 7-60.) *Winter and Spring.* The Euboeans and Lesbians apply to Agis, who resolves to aid the Lesbians. The Chians and Erythraeans apply to Lacedaemon; they are assisted by Tissaphernes, who is in difficulty about the tribute due to the king.

B.C.	OL.	
412.	91.4.	Pharnabazus also applies to Lacedaemon, inviting a fleet to the Hellespont. Alliance between Chios and Lacedaemon.
	92.1.	*Summer.* Conference of the allies at Corinth. The fleet is to sail first to Chios, then to Lesbos, then to the Hellespont. The Athenians take ships from the Chians as a pledge of fidelity. The Isthmian games.
		The Lacedaemonian fleet driven into Peiraeum by the Athenians, and there blockaded. Alcibiades urges the Lacedaemonians to persevere.
		Chios, Erythrae, and Clazomenae openly revolt from Athens. The Athenians determine to use their reserve of money and send a fleet to Asia.
		Revolt of Miletus. Alliance of the Lacedaemonians and Tissaphernes.
		The Lacedaemonian ships escape from Peiraeum and proceed to Asia.
		Great revolution at **Samos**; 200 nobles slain and 400 banished; distribution of land. A Democracy established, and the island declared independent.
		Revolt of Mytilene and Methymna in Lesbos, but the island is recovered; also Clazomenae. Distress of the Chians, whose territory is ravaged by the Athenians.
		Victory of the Athenians at Miletus; arrival of reinforcements from the Peloponnesians, Hermocrates of Syracuse with them.
		Winter. Suspicious conduct of Tissaphernes. Second treaty between Persia and Lacedaemon.
		Syracuse adopts an extreme form of democracy; the lot being used in the election of magistrates. (Diod. xiii. 75.)
		Constitution and Laws of Diocles.
		Twenty-first year of the War. (Thuc. viii. 61-109.)
411.		**Chios blockaded by the Athenians**; desertion of the slaves, which are numerous. Revolt of

B.C.	OL.	
411.	92.1.	Rhodes. Alcibiades joins Tissaphernes and damages the Peloponnesians; he intrigues with the oligarchs of Samos for his recall. Action of Phrynichus, who outwits Alcibiades. **Peisander arrives at Athens from Samos, and proposes the return of Alcibiades.** Third treaty between Persia and Lacedaemon. Oropus betrayed to the Boeotians. The Lacedaemonians in the Hellespont; Abydus and Lampsacus revolt, but the latter is recovered. The Chians recover command of the sea. **Subversion of the democracy at Athens. Not more than 5000 to have a share in the government. A reign of terror. Creation of a board of five and of the 400.** The leaders in the revolution were **Antiphon, Phrynichus, and Theramenes.**
	92.2.	**Proposals for peace to Agis, who refuses them.** *Summer.* Embassy from Athens to Samos, where, however, the oligarchs are put down by the sailors. The army swears allegiance to the democracy. The Peloponnesians pass from Tissaphernes to Pharnabazus. Revolt of Byzantium. Alcibiades at Samos. Quarrel between the Peloponnesians and Tissaphernes. Alcibiades follows Tissaphernes to Aspendus. The Samians hearing of the revolution at Athens wish to sail there at once, but are restrained by Alcibiades. **The Oligarchs at Athens again attempt negotiations with Sparta. Assassination of Phrynichus and destruction of the fort of Eetioneia.** Revolt of Euboea. **The 400 abolished, the 5000 established. Alcibiades recalled. Antiphon executed.** The Peloponnesians at the Hellespont with Pharnabazus. Defeat of the Peloponnesians at Cynossema. Alcibiades returns to Samos, and Tissaphernes arrives at Ephesus (*autumn*).

B.C.	OL.	
411.	92.2.	*End of the History of Thucydides.*
Winter. Battles at Rhoeteum and Abydus.
Tissaphernes at the Hellespont; he takes Alcibiades prisoner to Sardis.
Evagoras establishes himself at Salamis, in Cyprus.
The "*Lysistrata*" and "*Thesmophoriazusae*" of Aristophanes.
410.		*Twenty-second year of the War.* (Xen. Hell. i. 1, 11-37).
Alcibiades escapes and returns to the Hellespont, where he is joined by Theramenes and Thrasybulus, with their ships. The whole fleet follows Mindarus, the Spartan admiral, to Cyzicus.
Battle of Cyzicus; defeat of the Lacedaemonians and death of Mindarus. Alcibiades remains at Cyzicus twenty days collecting money.
On returning from Cyzicus the Athenians establish a fort (δεκατευτήριον) at Chrysopolis on the Bosporus to take tolls from ships passing through from the Pontus; and proceed to the Hellespont.
Pharnabazus supplies the Peloponnesians with money and wood. Ships are built at Antandros.
Hermocrates and the Syracusan generals deposed by orders from home; grief and indignation of their men. Hermocrates joins Pharnabazus.
Revolt at Thasos: the Lacedaemonian harmost driven out.
Thrasybulus at Athens; he repulses a sortie from Decelea. Agis desires Clearchus to be sent to Byzantium.
	92.3.	Thrasylus, with a fleet from Athens, defeats the Milesians at Pygela and invades Lydia, but he is subsequently defeated at Ephesus by Tissaphernes. He returns to Lampsacus and joins Alcibiades. Dissension between the two armies.
Evagoras, of Cyprus, rescues the island from the despotism of the Phoenician princes; restores Hellenic civilisation, and governs with great justice and mildness. He pays tribute to Persia.

B.C.	OL.	
410.	92.3.	Cyprus was perhaps less Hellenic than oriental, especially after the Ionian revolt, 496 B.C., so that it was abandoned by Pericles to the Persians. At a later time the Greek princes were supplanted by Phoenicians, and all Greeks were treated with great harshness.
409.		*Twenty-third year of the War.* (Xen. i. 2, 3.) Battle of Abydus, and repulse of Pharnabazus. Pylus reconquered by the Spartans; and Nisaea by the Megarians. Destruction of the colonists at Heraclea, and of the Lacedaemonian harmost by the Athenians and Oeteans. The Medes who had revolted from Darius now submit.
	92.4.	Alcibiades gains Selymbria and Chalcedon for Athens. Pharnabazus offers terms, and engages to conduct Athenian ambassadors to the king. In the absence of Clearchus, the Spartan commander, Byzantium is betrayed to the Athenians. Pharnabazus remains at Gordium, with the Athenian envoys, for the whole of the winter. Hannibal of Carthage invades Sicily, invited by a quarrel between the Selinuntines and Egestaeans. He takes Selinus and Himera by storm, and massacres the inhabitants. Hermocrates returns to Messene, and attempts to force his way into Syracuse. Failing in this he retires to Selinus (now desolate), from which, after fortifying it, he makes attacks on the Carthaginians in the neighbourhood. (Diod. xiii. 59, ff.)
408.		*Twenty-fourth year of the War.* (Xen. i. 4.) *Spring.* As the Athenian ambassadors proceed on their way to the king, they are met by the Lacedaemonian ambassadors returning from the king, who say that they have gained all that they require. Cyrus is with them, with power to carry on the war [ἄρξων πάντων τῶν

B.C.	OL.	
408.	92.4.	ἐπὶ θαλάττῃ καὶ ξυμπολεμήσων Λακεδαιμονίοις, κάρανον τῶν ἐς Καστωλὸν ἀθροιζομένων.] Pharnabazus retains the Athenian ambassadors for three years, and then sends them to the sea-coast.
Alcibiades prepares to return home, Thrasybulus reduces various towns in Thrace and Thasos; Thrasylus returns to Athens.
Lysander sent out by the Spartans in the room of Cratesippidas. He remains at Ephesus till Cyrus reaches Sardis, and there visits him.
	93.1.	**Alcibiades** chosen general, though still an exile. **He returns home on the Plynteria (Thargelion 25) amid the rejoicings of the citizens.**
Two months after he proceeds to Andros and Samos. (Xen. i. 4.)
Hermocrates again attempts to enter Syracuse, with the bones of the Syracusans who had been slain at Himera; though the feeling is strong in his favour, he is not admitted. On a third attempt he is defeated and slain. Among his adherents is Dionysius.
407.		*Twenty-fifth year of the War.* (Xen. i. 5.)
Cyrus co-operates with Lysander and raises the pay of the crews. He refuses to receive an embassy of Athenians. Lysander returns to Miletus and prepares his fleet.
During the absence of Alcibiades, Antiochus, who has been left in command, engages the fleet of Lysander and is defeated.
Battle of Notium. Alcibiades is deposed, and Conon is made commander of the fleet.
	93.2.	Lysander's year of office having come to an end, Callicratidas succeeds him. Cyrus receives him coldly, but, after obtaining money from Lacedaemon, Callicratidas attacks Methymna, and takes it. He refuses to sell the Methymnean captives (οὐκ ἔφη, ἑαυτοῦ γε ἄρχοντος, οὐδένα Ἑλλήνων ἐς τὸ κεῖνου δυνατὸν ἀνδραποδισθῆναι. Xen. i. 6, 14).

B.C.	OL.	
406.	93.2.	*Twenty-sixth year of the War.* (Xen. i. 6.)

Callicratidas defeats Conon at Mitylene, and shuts him up in the harbour with Leon and Erasinides, two of the Athenian generals.

Conon succeeds in sending out a ship, and the Athenians, hearing of his condition, send out 110 ships (ἐσβιβάζοντες τοὺς ἐν ἡλικίᾳ ὄντας ἅπαντας καὶ δούλους καὶ ἐλευθέρους.—Xen. i. 6, 24). With the contingent from Samos the fleet amounts to more than 150 ships. Callicratidas leaves 60 ships under Eteonicus at Mitylene and sails with 110 to meet the Athenian fleet.

Battle of Arginusae and defeat of the Peloponnesians. Death of Callicratidas.

The Athenian ships are unable, owing to a storm, to pick up the sailors on the disabled ships.

Eteonicus, hearing of the defeat, abandons Mitylene and retires to Chios. Conon is released. (Xen. i. 6.)

93.3. All the generals deposed except Conon.

(*N.B.*—Erasinides and Leon were at Mitylene with Conon, but Erasinides was certainly present at the battle of Arginusae. Leon is not mentioned in this matter by Xenophon. Six generals returned to Athens: Pericles, Diomedon, Lysias, Aristocrates, Thrasylus, and Erasinides. Protomachus and Aristogenes did not return.)

The Generals charged with misconduct. The six are put in prison by the council, and Theramenes attacks them in the assembly.

Popular feeling is excited against them, and by an illegal process they are condemned and put to death. (Xen. i. 7.)

Winter. The soldiers of Eteonicus at Chios form a conspiracy to seize the goods of the Chians. The conspiracy is discovered and suppressed. The Chians supply Eteonicus with money. Together with their allies at Ephesus, they send to Sparta with the request that Lysander may come out to them.

B.C.	OL.	
406.	93.3.	Second invasion of Sicily by the Carthaginians under Hannibal and Imilcon. Siege of Agrigentum, which is at length evacuated and plundered by the Carthaginians. Universal terror in Sicily. Dionysius revives the Hermocratean party, and becomes the tyrant of Syracuse. *Death of Sophocles and Euripides.*
405.		*Twenty-seventh year of the War.* (Xen. Hell. ii. 1.)
✗		**Lysander is sent out again as Epistoleus:** Aracus as admiral [ναύαρχος· οὐ γὰρ νόμος αὐτοῖς δὶς τὸν αὐτὸν ναυαρχεῖν]. On arriving at Ephesus, Lysander sends to Chios for Eteonicus and his ships, and collects as large a fleet as possible. Then he visits Cyrus and obtains money from him—Cyrus about this time is summoned to visit his father, who is sick. Lysander proceeds northwards with his fleet to Lampsacus, which he captures. **The Athenians follow, and finally take up a position at Aegospotami, opposite Lampsacus.** Lysander captures the Athenian ships and crews. Conon escapes with nine ships, one of which, the Paralus, carries the news to Athens.
	93.4.	The prisoners, 3000 in number, are put to death. All Hellas joins the Lacedaemonians, except Samos, which maintains a democracy. Lysander prepares to sail to Athens with 200 ships. Agis (from Decelea) and Pausanias (from Lacedaemon) march to the city. Lysander restores Aegina to the Aeginetans, and appears before Athens. **Athens, blockaded by land and sea, is reduced to a state of famine.** Ambassadors are sent to Agis to treat for peace; he bids them go to Lacedaemon. When sent thither the ephors, hearing the proposals, send them back from Sellasia.

B.C.	OL.	
405.	93.4.	Theramenes, on his own proposal, is sent to Lysander, who detains him three months and bids him go to Lacedaemon. Death of Darius II. Artaxerxes II. (Mnemon) succeeds (404-359). *The "Frogs" of Aristophanes.* Imilcon marches upon Gela. Dionysius marches to the relief of the city, but fails in an attack on the Carthaginian camp, and retires. Gela and Camarina evacuated and abandoned to the Carthaginians. Dionysius is accused of treachery, and an attempt is made to depose him, which he frustrates. Peace between Dionysius and the Carthaginians. (Diod. xiii. 114.) Dionysius fortifies Ortygia, and establishes himself strongly as despot of Syracuse. The redistribution of the Syracusan property among his friends, and exaction of money for his fortifications, provoke great discontent.
404.		**Theramenes sent to Sparta, with nine others, with full powers to conclude peace.** The Corinthians and Thebans urge the destruction of Athens; this the Spartans will not permit, but offer peace on the following conditions: **The Long walls and the Peiraeus to be pulled down; all the ships but twelve to be surrendered; the exiles to be received; the Athenians to have the same friends and enemies as the Lacedaemonians, and to follow them by land and sea wherever they lead.** The terms are accepted under pressure of famine. Lysander sails into the Peiraeus, the exiles return, the walls are pulled down to the sound of flutes, "for that day was thought to be the beginning of freedom for Hellas." (Xen. ii. 2.)
		SUPREMACY OF SPARTA. 404-379.
	94.1.	The Thirty established at Athens to revise the laws and constitution.

B.C.	OL.	
404.	94.1.	The Samians capitulate to Lysander, who restores the city to the oligarchs; establishes ten harmosts, and then disbands his fleet. With the Laconian ships he returns to Lacedaemon, taking with him the beaks of captured ships, all the Athenian triremes but twelve, a number of crowns received from grateful cities, and 470 talents of silver, the surplus of the funds furnished by Cyrus (τελευτῶντος τοῦ θέρους, ἐς ὃ ἑξάμηνος καὶ ὀκτὼ καὶ εἴκοσιν ἔτη τῷ πολέμῳ ἐτελεύτα.—Xen. ii. 3, 9).
		The Thirty neglect the reform of the constitution, and proceed to arrange the senate and offices to suit their own interests. All "sycophants" put to death. Lysander is requested to send a garrison to support them; and it is sent under the command of Callibius. With his help they arrest whom they please.
		A quarrel breaks out between Critias, one of the Thirty, and Theramenes, about their policy. Theramenes wishes for milder measures, and greater numbers in order to secure safety. Three thousand are selected as members of the government; the rest are deprived of their arms.
		Theramenes put to death at the instigation of Critias. (Xen. ii. 3.) A large number of citizens expelled, and their estates seized by the Thirty.
		Death of Alcibiades in Phrygia.
		Mutiny of the Syracusan army. Dionysius is besieged in Ortygia. With the help of Campanian mercenaries, Dionysius is victorious, and strengthens his position yet more.
403.		**Thrasybulus with seventy followers proceeds to Phyle.** The Thirty attack him, but are driven away by a thunderstorm. They send the Lacedaemonian garrison to besiege Phyle, but Thrasybulus defeats them, and, with now about a hundred men, comes to Peiraeus.
		The Thirty, wishing to secure Eleusis as a place of retreat, arrest and condemn to death three hundred of the inhabitants. (Xen. iii. 4, 8.)
		Critias is slain.

B.C.	OL.	
403.	94.2.	The Thirty are deposed, and retire to Eleusis. Ten officers chosen to manage the affairs of the city. Preparations are made for a battle between Peiraeus and the city. The Thirty send to Sparta for assistance. Lysander sends them money, comes to Eleusis, and his brother Libys supports him with a fleet. But Pausanias, the Lacedaemonian king, takes out a force and encamps near Peiraeus, intending to frustrate Lysander. After some fighting, he enters into secret negotiations with the Athenians in Peiraeus. **An embassy is sent to Sparta; and peace is restored with an amnesty to all but the Thirty, the Eleven, and the Ten in Peiraeus.** An attack is made on Eleusis. The leaders are slain; the rest received as citizens. A general amnesty (Xen. ii. 4). The Areopagus is restored; the laws are to be revised; the alphabet receives its final form. Dionysius is supported by Sparta. Lysander at Syracuse.
402.	94.3.	Cyrus sends to Sparta for assistance against his brother Artaxerxes. Samius, the Spartan admiral, is ordered to co-operate with him. Sailing to Cilicia, he prevents Syennesis from opposing Cyrus. (Xen. iii. 1.)
401.		Xenophon in the service of Cyrus. **Battle of Cunaxa, and death of Cyrus.**
	94.4.	**Return of the Ten Thousand to Trapezus.** (Xen., *Anabasis*). The Lacedaemonians, having for various reasons a grudge against the Eleans, send ambassadors to Elis, and demand that the neighbouring cities should be independent: ὅτι τοῖς τέλεσι τῶν Λακεδαιμονίων δίκαιον δοκοίη εἶναι, ἀφιέναι αὐτοὺς τὰς περιοικίδας πόλεις αὐτονόμους (Xen. iii. 2. 23). Agis invades Elis, but owing to an earthquake retires. Dionysius conquers Naxus, Catana, and Leontini.

B.C.	OL.	
400.	94.4.	Agis again invades Elis with all the Lacedaemonian allies, except the Boeotians and Corinthians, and with the Athenians. He is joined by a number of towns. He proceeds to Olympia and sacrifices to Zeus. Then he lays waste the country, and carries off abundant booty; καὶ ἐγένετο αὕτη ἡ στρατεία ὥσπερ ἐπισιτισμὸς τῇ Πελοποννήσῳ (Xen. iii. 2. 26). Arriving at Elis he ravages the suburbs, but does not take the city, though a party attempted to put it into his hands. He retires to Lacedaemon, leaving a garrison under Lysippus, at Epitalium, which continues to ravage the country.
		THE LACEDAEMONIANS IN ASIA. 400-394.
	95.1.	**Tissaphernes is made Satrap of Sardis** (as before), and of the provinces of Cyrus (ὧν τε αὐτὸς πρόσθεν ἦρχε, καὶ ὧν Κῦρος. Xen. iii. 1-3). He attempts to reduce the Ionian cities to subjection; they send to Lacedaemon for protection. **Thimbron** is sent out as **harmost** (with 1000 neodamodes, 4000 of the rest of the Peloponnesians, and 300 cavalry from Athens, of the horse of the Thirty). Xen. iii. 1.
		Preparations at Syracuse for attacking the Carthaginians. Fortification of Epipolae.
399.		The Eleans send to Lacedaemon to ask for peace. They are compelled to give up their cities, but are allowed to retain the management of the Olympian Games. (Xen. iii. 2, *end*.)
	95.2.	**Agis falls sick at Delphi, returns to Lacedaemon, and dies. Agesilaus**, his brother, though lame, succeeds; his son, Leotychides, being rejected as illegitimate.
		Thimbron is joined by the remnant of the Ten Thousand.
		He receives Pergamum, Teuthrania, and Halisarna (cities governed by the descendants of Demaratus of Sparta), and is joined by Gorgion and Gongylus (the first, ruler of Gambrium and Palaegambrium, the second, of Myrsina and Grynium, cities which had been given to Gongylus, a Medizing Eretrian), and captures other cities. He fails to take Larissa, and is ordered to Caria. Xen. iii. 1.

B.C.	OL.	
399.	95.2.	At Ephesus, he finds himself superseded by Dercyllidas (ἀνὴρ δοκῶν εἶναι μάλα μηχανικὸς, καὶ ἐπικαλεῖτο δὲ Σίσυφος. Xen. iii. 1, 8). Thimbron returns home, is fined, and banished.
		Dercyllidas comes to terms with Tissaphernes, and invades the territory of Pharnabazus, with whom he had had a previous quarrel when harmost at Abydus. He proceeds to Aeolis, a part of the satrapy of Pharnabazus, till lately governed by Mania, the widow of the late satrap, who had been recently assassinated by Midias, her son-in-law. Many of the cities come over to Dercyllidas.
		Dercyllidas takes Cebren, and, with the assistance of Midias, Scepsis, and Gergis, he possesses himself of the treasures of Mania. He comes to terms with Pharnabazus. Dercyllidas retires to Bithynian Thrace for the winter.
		Conspiracy of Cinadon, which reveals widespread discontent at Sparta. The ephors, receiving information, send Cinadon to Aulon, where he is arrested with certain helots. He is brought to Lacedaemon and put to death with torture.
		Not many Spartans were concerned in the plot, but the conspirators relied on the Helots, Neodamodes, Hypomeiones, and Perioeci (ὅπου γὰρ ἐν τούτοις τις λόγος γένοιτο περὶ Σπαρτιατῶν, οὐδένα δύνασθαι κρύπτειν τὸ μὴ οὐχ ἡδέως ἂν καὶ ὠμῶν ἐσθίειν αὐτῶν. Xen. iii. 3, 6).
		Death of Socrates.
		The Socratic school: Eucleides, Antisthenes, Aristippus, Plato. (Plato died 348 B.C., aged 81, or 82, and was therefore born in 430 or 429.)
398.	95.3.	**Dercyllidas** proceeds to Lampsacus, where he is visited by commissioners from Sparta, **and continued in his command for another year.** He continues the truce with Pharnabazus, and passes over to the Chersonesus, which he protects from the Thracians by building a wall from sea to sea (ἀρξάμενος ἀπὸ ἠρινοῦ χρόνου, and finished πρὸ ὀπώρας. Xen. iii. 2. 10). Then he returns to Asia.
		Philoxenus, Timotheus, and Telestes, the dithyrambic poets.

B.C.	OL.	
398.	95.3.	Great naval preparations at Syracuse; quadriremes and quinquiremes now built for the first time.
397.		Dercyllidas encamps round Atarneus and besieges it for eight months. Then he departs to Ephesus. He is ordered to Caria to attack Tissaphernes.
	95.4.	Tissaphernes and Pharnabazus unite, and proceed into Ionia, where they are followed by Dercyllidas, but a battle is avoided. Dercyllidas demands the liberation of the Greek cities in Asia; Tissaphernes and Pharnabazus the removal of the Greek forces and the Lacedaemonian harmosts. (Xen. iii. 2.) [Dercyllidas is now superseded by Agesilaus, who sent him as ambassador to Tissaphernes; as we next hear of him (Xen. iv. 3) at Amphipolis, he probably returned to Europe.]
		Xenophon and Philistus, the historians.
		Double marriage of Dionysius. The Carthaginians at Syracuse are plundered by the permission of Dionysius. He marches against Motye and besieges it. General massacre of the Carthaginians in Sicily.
396.		**Great alarm raised at Sparta by Herodas, who reports that a large fleet is being prepared in Phoenicia (300 sail), the destiny of which was unknown.** On the instigation of Lysander, **Agesilaus** undertakes a campaign in Asia [with 30 Spartans, 2000 neodamodes, and 6000 allies].
		Lysander offers to go with him to restore the "decarchies," which had been removed by the ephors in favour of hereditary forms of government.
	96.1.	**Agesilaus sets out for Asia;** the Boeotarchs will not allow him to sacrifice at Aulis (in imitation of Agamemnon). He passes to Geraestus and Ephesus.
		Tissaphernes inquires why Agesilaus has come. On learning that he wishes to secure the independence of the Greeks, he proposes a truce, in order to consult the king. This is agreed to, but Tissaphernes immediately breaks faith by sending for reinforcements.

B.C.	OL.	
396.	96.1.	Dissension between Agesilaus and Lysander. Lysander is sent to the Hellespont, where he persuades Spithridates to revolt from Pharnabazus, and brings him to Agesilaus. (Xen. iii. 4.)
		Tissaphernes declares war on Agesilaus, who invades Phrygia and carries off much spoil. Repulse of the Greek cavalry by the Persian horse of Pharnabazus in the neighbourhood of Dascylium. Agesilaus retires to the sea-coast, and prepares a body of cavalry. (Xen. iii. 4.)
		After a vigorous resistance, Motye is taken. Imilcon arrives with a great force from Carthage, and retakes it. Dionysius retires to Syracuse.
395.		In the spring Agesilaus collects his army at Ephesus—where he exercises and trains them; the whole city busy with warlike preparations (πολέμου ἐργαστήριον). To inspire contempt for the enemy, he orders some captives to be stripped and sold. (Xen. iii. 4, 19.)
		Lysander and the thirty Spartans recalled, and replaced by Herippidas and others.
		Agesilaus marches on Sardis. An engagement takes place on the Pactolus; the Persian camp is taken with booty to the amount of seventy talents and some camels, which Agesilaus sent to Greece.
		Tissaphernes put to death by Tithraustes, who is sent to succeed him. Tithraustes offers terms to Agesilaus: the Asiatic cities are to be independent on condition of paying their old quota to the king. Agesilaus refers to the authorities at Sparta, and meantime undertakes to retire into Phrygia (in the satrapy of Pharnabazus), if Tithraustes will support his forces. He is made head of the fleet as well as of the army, and orders the cities to build ships. (Xen. iii. 4.)
		Tithraustes, perceiving that Agesilaus has no intention of leaving Asia, sends Timocrates of Rhodes into Greece, with fifty talents, to disburse among the leaders of the various cities in order to stir up war against Lacedaemon. Timocrates visits Thebes, Corinth, Argos. The Athenians need no bribes.

B.C.	OL.	
395.	96.1.	The Thebans persuade the Opuntian Locrians to devastate the debateable ground between themselves and the Phocians. The Phocians at once invade Locris, and make reprisals. The Thebans aid the Locrians, and the Phocians appeal to Lacedaemon.
		The Lacedaemonians, eager to make war on Thebes, send Lysander to Phocis, where Pausanias is to join him and Haliartus. The Thebans ask aid from Athens.
		Lysander attacks Haliartus, and is slain. Pausanias arrives, and the Athenian contingent joins the Thebans.
		The Peloponnesians retire from Boeotia without a battle. Pausanias, on his return home, is condemned to death; he goes to exile in Tegea.
		Autumn.—Agesilaus in Phrygia, which he lays waste; he is persuaded by Spithridates to go into Paphlagonia, where the king Cotys becomes his ally. He negotiates a marriage between the daughter of Spithridates and the son of Cotys. He marches to Dascylium, and encamps in the neighbourhood of Pharnabazus' palace, who wanders through the country, fearing to be besieged. Spithridates and the Paphlagonians abandon Agesilaus, and go to Ariaeus, at Sardis (Xen. iv. 1), being refused a share in the spoil of Pharnabazus' camp, which had been attacked and taken by Herippidas.
		Agesilaus and Pharnabazus are reconciled by the good offices of Apollophanes of Cyzicus, a common friend. Agesilaus undertakes to leave the country, and not to ravage it for the future.
		Messene taken by the Carthaginians, who are also victorious in a great naval battle off Catana. Dionysius retires again to Syracuse; Imilcon occupies the great harbour, and plunders Achradina.
		Alliance of Sparta and Dionysius.
		A pestilence breaks out in the Carthaginian army, which is now severely defeated and almost destroyed. Imilcon leads away the Carthaginians under a secret treaty, and starves himself to death.

B.C.	OL.	
394.	96.2.	**394–387. CORINTHIAN WAR.**

Agesilaus leaves Phrygia about the beginning of spring (σχεδὸν δέ καὶ ἔαρ ἤδη ὑπέφαινεν. Xen. iv. 1. 41), and encamps in the plain of Thebe, intending to collect a great army and march up the country.

The Lacedaemonians send Epicydidas to recall Agesilaus. He leaves Euxenus as harmost, with 4000 men, behind, crosses the Hellespont, and taking with him picked men of his army, enters Greece by the route taken by Xerxes. (Xen. iv. 2.)

Meanwhile the Lacedaemonians march out under Aristodemus the guardian of Agesipolis, to Sicyon. The allies take up a position at Nemea. (Numbers on each side: Lacedaemonians and their allies, 13,500 infantry, 600 Lacedaemonian horse, 300 Cretan bowmen, 4000 slingers. Athenians and their allies: 24,000 infantry, 1550 horse, with many light-armed soldiers.) **Battle of Nemea.** The Lacedaemonians are victorious over the Athenians and finally defeat the whole allied army. (*July.*)

96.3. News of the victory is brought to Agesilaus at Amphipolis by Dercyllidas, who is bidden to announce it in Asia. Agesilaus passes through Macedonia into Thessaly, which he crosses with some difficulty, and reaches Boeotia to meet the allies.

News is now brought to him of the **defeat of Peisander** (his brother-in-law, whom he had made commander of the fleet) **by Conon at Cnidos.** (*August.*)

Pharnabazus and Conon, after their victory, remove the Lacedaemonian harmosts from the cities on the sea-coast. Dercyllidas, now harmost of Abydus, maintains his ground. Pharnabazus, after invading the territory of Abydus, commissions Conon to get together as many ships as possible for the next year and goes home. (Xen. iv. 7.)

Battle of Coronea. The most important in Xenophon's time (οἵα οὐκ ἄλλη τῶν γ' ἐφ' ἡμῶν. Xen. iv. 3. 16). Agesilaus is victorious; he devotes a tenth of the spoil (= 100 talents) to Apollo at Delphi. Gylis, the polemarch, while invading Locris, is slain. (*August.*)

B.C.	OL.	
394.	96.3.	The army is disbanded; Agesilaus returns home. Reestablishment of Messene (in Sicily) by Dionysius, who is, however, repulsed before Tauromenium.
		Lysias, the orator.
		Strattis, the comedian.
393.		In the spring Pharnabazus and Conon sail to Lacedaemon, and capture Cythera. Pharnabazus returns home; **Conon rebuilds the walls**
	96.4.	**of Athens with the help of Persian money and ships.**
		Iphicrates at Phlius; he defeats the citizens with such slaughter that they send to Lacedaemon for aid; and ravages Arcadia, where his peltasts inspire great terror. (Xen. iv. 4. 15.)
392.		Division of feeling at Corinth. The nobles wish to come to terms with Lacedaemon; in consequence the demos massacre many of them, on the last day of the festival of Eucleia. Two of the party admit Praxitas, the Lacedaemonian commander, who is stationed at Sicyon, into the walls leading to Lechaeum.
		Battle of Lechaeum. Victory of the Lacedaemonians, and great slaughter of the Argives, who had come to the rescue of Lechaeum. Praxitas takes and garrisons Sidus, and Crommyon, and fortifies Epieikia; destroys the walls in part, then retires towards Lacedaemon.
		The Lacedaemonians, under Agesilaus, invade Corinth, and establish themselves at the Peiraeum, about the time of the Isthmian games, which in this year are celebrated once by the Corinthian exiles (the aristocrats) and once by the Argives (as representing the Corinthian people). While at Peiraeum news is **brought to Agesilaus that a mora has been cut to pieces by Iphicrates.**
	97.1.	The mora, 600 strong, had gone out from Lechaeum to set the Amycleans, who were returning home to the Hyacinthia, on their way. On its return Callias and Iphicrates issue from Corinth, and slay about 250 men. (Xen. iv. 5.)

B.C.	OL.	
392.	97.1.	Agesilaus conducts back the remnant home as much as possible by night. Iphicrates recaptures Sidus and Crommyon, and Oenoe, which Agesilaus had fortified.
		Xenarchus, the son of Sophron, the writer of Mimes.
		Dionysius fails to take Rhegium, and concludes a peace for one year.
		The Lacedaemonians send Antalcidas to Tiribazus, the general of the king, to propose peace. The Athenians send Conon and others to operate against them. Neither side succeeds, but Tiribazus puts Conon in prison.
		The "Ecclesiazusae" of Aristophanes.
391.		The Achaeans of Calydon, attacked by the Acarnanians (and their allies, the Athenians and Thebans) apply to Lacedaemon for help. Agesilaus is sent out; he threatens to lay waste the whole country unless the Acarnanians renounce their allies and join the Lacedaemonians. They refuse, and he continues to ravage the country till the autumn, and returns home by Rhium. (Xen. iv. 6.)
		Peace concluded between Dionysius and the Carthaginians under Magon.
	97.2.	The Athenians help to rebuild the walls of Corinth reaching to Lechaeum.
		Agesilaus invades Argolis; then, passing into Corinth, captures the newly restored walls. His brother Teleutias supports him by sea.
		Strouthas, who has succeeded Tiribazus as the general of the Persian forces, warmly aids the Athenians. Thimbron is sent by the Spartans against him, but he is defeated and killed.
		Dionysius captures Tauromenium.
		Andocides, the orator.
		Plato, the comic poet.
390.		Agesilaus is preparing to invade Acarnania again, but the Acarnanians send an embassy to Sparta, and enter into alliance with them.

B.C.	OL.	
390.	97.2.	The Lacedaemonians, wishing to aid the Rhodian aristocrats against the Athenians and democratic party, send Ecdicus with eight ships and Diphridas. Diphridas passes over into Asia and achieves success there. Ecdicus is succeeded by Teleutias, with twenty-seven ships. He defeats Philocrates, the Athenian, who is sailing with ten triremes to aid Evagoras against Persia. (Xen. iv. 8.) The Athenians send out Thrasybulus, to sea. He sails to the Hellespont, and establishes the Athenian influence in that direction. At Byzantium he sells the tax of a tenth on the ships sailing through from Pontus, and establishes a democracy in the city. He also brings over the cities of Lesbos to Athens after defeating the Lacedaemonian harmost. At Aspendus he is slain by some of the citizens.
	97.3.	
		Dionysius attacks Rhegium, but without success, his fleet being ruined by a storm. Great defeat of the Thurians by the Lucanians.
389.		Dercyllidas is replaced at Abydus by Anaxibius. The Athenians send Iphicrates to the Hellespont; who defeats and slays Anaxibius.
		The Lacedaemonians resolve to invade Argos. [Agesipolis consults the oracle at Olympia and Delphi, whether he may disregard the sacred truce pleaded by wilful miscalculation of months by the Argives. Xen. iv. 7.] He disregards the truce and an earthquake, but after greatly damaging the Argives is compelled to retire by unfavourable omens. (Xen. iv. 7.)
		Death of Conon in Cyprus.
	97.4.	The Aeginetans at war with Athens. They are supported by Teleutias, who is succeeded by Hierax.
		Antalcidas sent out as admiral by the Lacedaemonians. He goes to Ephesus, and joins Tiribazus.
		Chabrias passes over into Aegina, attacks Gorgopas, the Spartan leader there; defeats and slays him. The Aeginetans are again supported by Teleutias, who makes an attack on the Peiraeus, and carries off much booty. (Xen. v. 1.)

B.C.	OL.	
389.	97.4.	Amyntas II., king of Macedonia. Dionysius attacks the Italiot Greeks, who are defeated and captured.
388.	98.1.	Antalcidas returns with Tiribazus, and collects a large fleet in the neighbourhood of the Hellespont, with which he prevents the corn ships from sailing to Athens. This makes the Athenians inclined for peace. Chabrias in Cyprus with Evagoras, who conquers Tyre and Cilicia. *The "Plutus" of Aristophanes.*
387.		**Peace concluded between the Greeks and Artaxerxes Mnemon. Peace of Antalcidas.**
	98.2.	**The conditions were: that the cities of Asia should belong to the king, with Cyprus and Clazomenae; the remaining Hellenic states, great and small, are to be independent. Lemnos, Imbros, and Scyros still to be the property of the Athenians.** (Xen. *Hell.* v. 1. 25, 26.) The Thebans at first refuse to restore independence to the Boeotian cities, but are compelled by Agesilaus to do so; the Argives also are not allowed to remain in Corinth, which is thus brought under the influence of the Lacedaemonians.
386.		Plataea is restored, under Lacedaemonian influence. The city becomes "a dependency of Sparta," Thespiae and Orchomenus are garrisoned by Sparta, and parties favourable to Sparta are established in all the towns of Boeotia. (Xen. v. 4. 46.)
	98.3.	Leucon, prince of the Hellespont.
		386-361. SPARTA AND THEBES.
385.	98.4.	The Mantineans are compelled by the Spartans to pull down their walls; they are broken up into four villages ($\kappa\alpha\theta\acute{\alpha}\pi\epsilon\rho$ $\tau\grave{o}$ $\dot{\alpha}\rho\chi\alpha\hat{\iota}o\nu$ $\ddot{\omega}\kappa o\hat{\upsilon}\nu$) each of which receives a Lacedaemonian commander ($\xi\epsilon\nu\alpha\gamma\acute{o}\varsigma$).

B.C.	OL.	
385.	98.4.	The thirty years' truce after the battle of Mantinea had now come to an end, and the Lacedaemonians took occasion of the general disarming of Hellas, to crush any one against whom they had grudges. Agesilaus begs to be excused from this campaign, on account of the services rendered to his father by the Mantineans; Agesipolis undertakes it. He builds a wall round the city, but is unable to take it till, by blocking up the river and causing it to overflow, he saps the foundations of the walls. The Argive party are allowed to leave the city unharmed, owing to the good offices of Pausanias, the father of Agesipolis, who is still living in exile (Xen. v. 2) and who had been on friendly terms with the Mantineans. The siege was after the harvest (αἰσθόμενος ὅτι ὁ σῖτος ἐν τῇ πόλει πολὺς εἴη, εὐετηρίας γενομένης τῷ πρόσθεν ἔτει, i.e. in the preceding Olympiad, 98.3.) Dionysius restores Alcetas to Epirus; his attempt on Delphi is prevented by Sparta.
384.	99.1.	March of the Spartans to Epirus against the Illyrians. Lysias at Olympia: he points out the danger of the Greeks from the Persians and Dionysius of Syracuse. The tent of Dionysius, remarkable for its magnificence, is attacked. (Grote, vii. 67.) *Ctesias, the historian.* *Birth of Aristotle.*
383.	99.2.	The oligarchical exiles of Phlius present themselves at Lacedaemonia and ask to be restored. The Lacedaemonians send to Phlius and demand their restoration, to which the Phliasians agree. The property of the exiles is restored. (Xen. v. 1.)

383-379. Sparta at War with Olynthus.

Ambassadors from Acanthus and Apollonia appear at Sparta, asking assistance against Olynthus. They plead:—
(1.) The aggression of Olynthus, who has become the head of a great confederacy, and is now attacking Macedonia, and compelling cities to join her. Her forces amount to 800 hoplites and many more peltasts, and nearly 1000 horse.

B.C.	OL.	
383.	99.2.	(2.) The fear that Athens, Boeotia, and Olynthus may coalesce. Negotiations are already on foot.
		(3.) The growth of Olynthian power or influence in Chalcidice, Boeotia, and Thrace (in which case the mines of Pangaeum would be in their control).
		The Spartans determine on war with Olynthus. A force of 10,000 is to be raised, and those who do not wish to serve in person are to send money (3 Aeginetan obols per man, and 12 obols for a horseman).
		The Acanthians press for immediate assistance. The Spartans send Eudamidas with 2000 neodamodes, perioeci, and skiritae. Phoebidas, the brother of Eudamidas, is to follow with the larger force.
		Phoebidas at Thebes. The Thebans separated into factions, which are headed by the two polemarchs, Ismenias and Leontiades. Ismenias is opposed to the Lacedaemonians; Leontiades favours them.
		With the help of Leontiades, Phoebidas seizes the Cadmea (the acropolis of Thebes).
		Ismenias is put in prison; 400 of his adherents leave for Athens. Leontiades goes to Sparta, where, after some discussion, the act of Phoebidas is allowed, and judges are sent to try Ismenias. Ismenias is condemned and put to death.
		Dionysius renews the war with Carthage. At first he is victorious, Magon and many Carthaginians being slain; but at length the Carthaginians totally defeat him, and he is compelled to accept their terms, giving up a large amount of territory and paying 1000 talents.
382.		Teleutias is sent out with a part of the 10,000 to Olynthus. He collects as many forces as possible, and is joined by Derdas, the chief of the Elimiotes. In an engagement, the Lacedaemonians, with the help of Derdas, repulse the Olynthians.

B.C.	OL.	
382.	99.2.	This was before the summer, *i.e.* the summer of 382. For the rest of the year little was done. (Xen. v. 2, *end.*) *Birth of Demosthenes.* *Isocrates and Isaeus, orators.*
381.		In the spring the Olynthians, making a raid on Apollonia, are repulsed by Derdas.
	99.4.	Later, Teleutias and the Lacedaemonians are entirely defeated by the Olynthians. Teleutias is slain; his army dispersed. (Xen. v. 3.) Agesipolis is sent out with a large force from Sparta. Thirty Spartans accompany him.
380.		He is joined by many perioeci, and trophimi, and by Thessalian horse. Amyntas and Derdas support him. But he was seized
	100.1.	with a fever (it was now midsummer) and died at Aphytis. Polybiades is sent out in his place. Evagoras of Cyprus, after a war of ten years, comes to terms with the Persians. He is soon afterwards assassinated. **Phlius besieged by Agesilaus.** The Phliasians, reflecting that Agesipolis was now absent from Sparta, and that both kings could not be absent at one time, refuse to carry out the terms agreed upon with the exiles. The exiles repair to Lacedaemon, and on their return are fined. Agesilaus marches out, and besieges Phlius.
379.		The Phliasians still hold out, but at length supplies fail, and they send to Sparta to surrender their city to the authorities. Agesilaus regards this as a slight, but the city refers the terms to him. Fifty of the restored exiles and fifty of the men in the city are to decide who is to live and who is
	100.2.	to be put to death, and to draw up a constitution. The whole siege had occupied a year and eight months. (Xen. v. 4.) **Olynthus surrenders to Polybiades.** The terms are: that the Olynthians must have the same friends and enemies as the Lacedaemonians, follow their leadership, and be their allies. **The liberation of Thebes.**

B.C.	OL.	
379.	100.2.	The Theban exiles from Athens, seven in number, of whom Mellon was chief (so Xenophon, omitting all mention of Pelopidas), succeed in entering Thebes with the connivance of Phyllidas, the secretary of Archias and the polemarchs. Disguised as women, they are brought into the presence of Archias and others, and slay them. Next they proceed to the house of Leontiades, and put him to death, and to the gaol, where they liberate the prisoners. They proclaim that the tyrants are dead, and bid the Thebans join them. On the next day they sent word to two of the Athenian generals of their success; and with their help they attempt the acropolis, which surrenders, the Spartan harmost and his men being allowed to depart in their arms. The harmost is put to death in Sparta, and war declared against the Thebans.
		Agesilaus refuses to go on the expedition to Thebes, pleading his age. Cleombrotus, the successor of Agesipolis, is sent (his first campaign, in the winter: $\mu\acute{a}\lambda a\ \chi\epsilon\iota\mu\hat{\omega}\nu os\ \ddot{o}\nu\tau os$. Xen. v. 4. 14.)
		The Athenians put to death one of the generals who assisted the Thebans, and banish the other.
378.		First invasion of Boeotia by the Lacedaemonians under Cleombrotus.
		As the way by Eleutherae is secured by Chabrias with Athenian peltasts, Cleombrotus proceeds to Plataea and Thespiae. He advances to Cynoscephalae, and then returns to Thespiae, where he leaves Sphodrias as harmost, with one-third of his forces and money. Then he returns home, "having done as little damage as possible." (Xen. v. 4. 16.) On his way home he is encountered by a violent wind (near Creusis), so that his soldiers are unable to carry their arms.
		Attempt of Sphodrias on the Peiraeus.
		Sphodrias, being left in Thespiae, endeavours to seize Peiraeus. He fails in the attempt, and is put on his trial at Lacedaemon, but allowed to escape: $\kappa a\grave{\iota}\ \pi o\lambda\lambda o\hat{\iota}s\ \ddot{\epsilon}\delta o\xi\epsilon\nu\ a\ddot{\upsilon}\tau\eta\ \delta\grave{\eta}\ \dot{\epsilon}\nu\ \Lambda a\kappa\epsilon\delta a\iota\mu o\nu\acute{\iota}o\iota s\ \dot{a}\delta\iota\kappa\acute{\omega}\tau a\tau a\ \delta\acute{\iota}\kappa\eta\ \kappa\rho\iota\theta\hat{\eta}\nu a\iota.$ (Xen. v. 4. 24.)
		The Athenians build gates to the Peiraeus, and ships, and join the Boeotians against Sparta.

B.C.	OL.	
378.	100.3.	Second invasion of Boeotia by the Lacedaemonians, under Agesilaus.
He secures the passes of Cithaeron by the help of a band of Cleitorian mercenaries. He finds the Theban territory strongly secured, and finally, leaving Phoebidas at Thespiae, returns home.
Phoebidas continues to ravage the country, but is slain by the Theban cavalry.
The Theban cause is now in the ascendant, and the δῆμος from the various neighbouring cities flocks to Thebes.
[ὁ μέντοι δῆμος ἐξ αὐτῶν εἰς τὰς Θήβας ἀπεχώρει· ἐν πάσαις γὰρ ταῖς πόλεσι δυναστεῖαι καθειστήκεσαν, ὥσπερ ἐν Θήβαις, ὥστε καὶ οἱ ἐν ταύταις ταῖς πόλεσι φίλοι τῶν Λακεδαιμονίων βοηθείας ἐδέοντο. Xen. v. 4. 16.]
The Lacedaemonians send a polemarch and a mora to Thespiae, and rebuild Plataea.
Reform of Finance at Athens.
Arrangement of all property in classes; so that in each class the amount taxed (τίμημα) stood in a certain proportion to the whole amount possessed. The whole τίμημα amounted to about 6000 talents.
Arrangement of symmories for the collection of the tax; 20 symmories of 60 citizens each = 1200, among whom 300 were the wealthiest. This arrangement was also extended to the trierarchies.
The second Confederacy of Delos.
Chabrias, Timotheus, and Callistratus formed the second confederacy. Athens to be the president and meeting-place; but every member to be autonomous, and have one vote. No Athenian citizen to hold property in the territory of the confederates.
377.	100.4.	*Spring* (ἐπεὶ τὸ ἔαρ ἐπέστη. Xen. v. 4. 47).
Third invasion of Boeotia by the Lacedaemonians, under Agesilaus.
He ravages the country towards the east of Thebes, and makes a feint of attacking the city. He finds dissensions at Thespiae, which he composes, and returns home.

B.C.	OL.	
377.	100.4.	The Thebans, distressed by the destruction of their harvests, obtain corn from Pagasae. On his return home Agesilaus meets with an accident which incapacitates him for service.
376.		Fourth invasion of Boeotia by the Peloponnesians, under Cleombrotus. Spring (ἐπεὶ ἔαρ ὑπέφαινε, Xen. v. 4, 59). Unable to force his way over Cithaeron he retires. The Lacedaemonian allies are dissatisfied at the conduct of the war. A fleet of sixty triremes is sent out under Pollis, which cuts off the Athenian corn supply from the north.
	101.1.	**The fleet is defeated at Naxos by the Athenians under Chabrias.**
375.		At the request of the Thebans, the Athenians send a fleet under Timotheus to ravage the coast of Peloponnesus. He takes Corcyra, and defeats the Spartans under Nicolochus at Alyzia. Timotheus, remaining at Corcyra, adds to and refits his fleet. (Xen. v. 4, *end.*) The Thebans recover many of the neighbouring towns (ἅτε δὲ εἰς τὰς Θήβας οὐκ ἐμβεβληκότων τῶν πολεμίων, οὔτ' ἐν ᾧ Κλεόμβροτος ἦγε τὴν στρατίαν ἔτει, οὔτ' ἐν ᾧ Τιμόθεος περιέπλευσε, θράσεως δὴ ἐστρατεύοντο οἱ Θηβαῖοι ἐπὶ τὰς περιοικίδας πόλεις, καὶ πάλιν αὐτὰς ἐλάμβανον —Xen. v. 4. 63).
	101.2.	**Rise of the power of Jason of Pherae.** Polydamas of Pharsalus appears at Sparta asking for assistance to enable him to resist the aggression of Jason, but the Spartans find themselves unable to give it. Polydamas, on his return, arranges that Pharsalus shall join Jason, who becomes Tagus of the Thessalians. He fixes the contingents for each city, and raises a force of 8000 horse, 20,000 hoplites, besides peltasts. The perioeci pay the same tribute that they did to Scopas. The Thebans invade Phocis—having now reduced all the cities in Boeotia. The Phocians apply to Lacedaemon for help. Cleombrotus is sent with four morae. The Thebans retire into their own country and guard the passes. (Xen. vi. 1, 2, *init.*)

B.C.	OL.	
375.	101.2.	Battle of Orchomenus, and defeat of the Lacedaemonians (who had left the town on a campaign into Locris) by Pelopidas and the Sacred Band. (Plutarch, Pelop. c. 17; Diod. xv. 37.)
374.	101.3.	The Athenians, perhaps jealous of the growing power of Thebes, are anxious to bring the war with Sparta to a close. An embassy sent to Sparta, and peace concluded, but it is immediately broken off. For Timotheus, when sailing back from Corcyra, being recalled according to the terms of the peace, replaces some exiles on the island of Zacynthus.
373.		The Zacynthians at once appeal to Lacedaemon. A large fleet is sent out under the command of Mnasippus, who sails to Corcyra, lays waste the country, and invests the city by land and sea. In his army were 1500 mercenaries. [Prosperous condition of Corcyra: ἐδῄου ἐξεργασμένην μὲν παγκάλως καὶ πεφυτευμένην τὴν χώραν, μεγαλοπρεπεῖς δὲ οἰκήσεις καὶ οἰνῶνας κατεσκευασμένους ἔχουσαν ἐπὶ τῶν ἀγρῶν· καὶ ἀνδράποδα δὲ καὶ βοσκήματα πάμπολλα ἡλίσκετο ἐκ τῶν ἀγρῶν. Xen. vi. 2.] The Athenians send Timotheus to aid Corcyra, but, dissatisfied with the time which he spends in collecting supplies, they supersede him, and send Iphicrates and Chabrias in his place.
372.		Meanwhile the Corcyreans succeed in defeating the Lacedaemonians, who are compelled to quit the island. Mnasippus is slain, and much of the booty and the sick abandoned. Iphicrates, arriving after the departure of the Lacedaemonians, captures nine out of ten ships sent by Dionysius to help them. His crews till the lands of the Corcyreans. He continues to prosecute the war in Acarnania, and finally takes his ships to the Lacedaemonian coast.

B.C.	OL.	
371.	102.1.	Plataea has been again destroyed by the Thebans, and Thespiae is in danger of a similar fate. This alarms the Athenians, who send to Lacedaemon with proposals for peace. Callias, Autocles, and Callistratus at Sparta. Peace is agreed upon. The harmosts are to be withdrawn from the cities; the fleets and armies to be disbanded, and the cities to be independent. (Xen. vi. 3, 18.) The Thebans demand that they shall be enrolled in the peace as Boeotians, not as Thebans. Agesilaus refuses. The Thebans are excluded from the peace.
	102.2.	Cleombrotus, who is still in Phocis, is ordered to attack the Thebans. **Battle of Leuctra.** **Defeat of the Spartans; death of Cleombrotus.** The news arrives at Sparta on the last day of the Gymnopaedia. When Cleombrotus inquired of the τέλη what he was to do, Prothous suggested that he should disband his army, and that they should send round to the cities to contribute a sum to the temple of Apollo (as much as each city wished), and if any city refused to allow autonomy the allies should assemble and make war upon it, ἡ δὲ ἐκκλησία, ἀκούσασα ταῦτα, ἐκεῖνον μὲν φλυαρεῖν ἡγήσατο, ἤδη γὰρ, ὡς ἔοικε, τὸ δαιμόνιον ἦγεν. (Xen. vi. 4.) Cleombrotus enters Boeotia through Thisbae, and advances to Creusis, where he captures the fort and takes twelve Theban vessels. Then he advances to Leuctra, the Thebans being on the hill opposite, near the tomb of the two girls who had been violated and killed by Lacedaemonians, which they thought to be an omen of victory. The camp-followers of the Boeotians, who wish to leave the camp, are driven back by the Peloponnesians. The cavalry of the Lacedaemonians very inferior to the Thebans, because the horses at Sparta were owned by wealthy men, who hired others to fight (τῶν δ' αὖ στρατιωτῶν οἱ τοῖς σώμασιν ἀδυνατώτατοι καὶ ἥκιστα φιλότιμοι ἐπὶ τῶν ἵππων ἦσαν). The Lacedaemonian infantry drawn up 12 deep, the Theban 15 deep.

B.C.	OL.	
371.	102.2.	The Lacedaemonian cavalry at once defeated and driven upon their infantry. The Thebans follow: the right, where Cleombrotus is, gives way. Dinon, the polemarch, is slain; Sphodrias and his son. The left also retires. Behind the trench which was in front of the camp they pitch their tents. Xenophon puts the number of the slain at 1000 Lacedaemonians, 400 Spartans out of 700. The Spartans ask for their dead under truce.
		The Thebans, eager to destroy the remnant of the Lacedaemonians, send to Athens where their messages are coldly received, and to Jason who dissuades them from their purpose. The Lacedaemonians retire by Creusis to Aegosthena, where they meet with the contingent which has been sent out under Archidamus, the son of Agesilaus, to support them.
370.		**Results of the Battle of Leuctra.**
	102.3.	(1) The Athenians send for all who wish to hold to the peace of Antalcidas, and this oath is taken: ἐμμενῶ ταῖς σπονδαῖς ἃς βασιλεὺς κατέπεμψε, καὶ τοῖς ψηφίσμασι τῶν Ἀθηναίων καὶ τῶν συμμάχων· ἐὰν δέ τις στρατεύηται ἐπί τινα πόλιν τῶν ὁμοσασῶν τόνδε τὸν ὅρκον, βοηθήσω παντὶ σθένει. (Xen. vi. 5.) The Eleans offer some objections, contesting the autonomy of the Marganeans, the Scilluntians and the Triphylians.
		(2) The Mantineans unite and rebuild their walls. Agesilaus attempts to defer the project, offering Lacedaemonian assistance. The Mantineans proceed with their work, and Agesilaus is unable to prevent it.
		(3) Party quarrels in Tegea. The democratic party wish for a united Arcadia, which shall manage the affairs of the nation (καὶ ὅτι νικῴη ἐν τῷ κοινῷ, τοῦτο κύριον εἶναι καὶ τῶν πόλεων). The aristocrats wish things to remain as they are. With the help of the Mantineans, the democrats put some of their opponents to death. 800 escape to Sparta.
		(4) **The Scytalism at Argos.** The democracy discover a plot of the oligarchs against the democracy. Outburst of popular fury, ending in the execution of 1200 of the principal citizens. (Diod. xv. 57, 58.) Other cities—Phigalea, Phlius, Corinth, Sicyon, Megara—are the scenes of like disturbances.

B.C.	OL.	
370.	102.3.	(5) Foundation of Megalopolis—which Xenophon does not expressly mention (Pausanias, Diodorus).
		(6) Massacres at Orchomenus in Boeotia by the Thebans. The males put to death, the women and children sold into slavery. (Diod. xv. 79.)
		The Spartans aid the Tegeate exiles. Agesilaus marches into Arcadia; he is joined by the Heraeans and Lepreatae. The Orchomenians (Arcadians) refuse to join the Arcadians; they are attacked by the Mantineans, but join Agesilaus, who cannot succeed in bringing the Mantineans to a battle, and returns (καὶ γὰρ ἦν μέσος χειμών, Xen. vi. 5. 20).
		Assassination of Jason of Pherae—before the Pythian games.
		Jason is succeeded by Polydorus, his brother, who is supposed to have instigated the murder. Polydorus is slain by Polyphron, another brother, who is again assassinated by Alexander of Pherae.
369.		The Thebans invade Peloponnesus for the first time.
		The Thebans join the Arcadians. With them are the Phocians, the Euboeans, the Locrians, the Acarnanians, the Heracliotae, the Malians, and horse and peltasts from Thessaly. They invade Laconia, burn Sellasia, and encamp near the city of Sparta, on the left of the river.
	102.4.	The Theban army passes to Amyclae, and there crosses the river; then, failing to take Sparta, passes down to Helos and Gythium.
		The Spartans arm the Helots (6000 came forward) and are assisted by the Phliasians, the Corinthians, the Epidaurians and Pellenians.
		The Thebans restore Messenia, and rebuild Messene (Pausanias iv. 27 ff., not mentioned by Xenophon).
		The Athenians conclude a peace with the Lacedaemonians, and send Iphicrates to prevent the return of the Thebans. This he fails to do: while he is watching on Oneum, they pass by Cenchreae. (Xen. vi. 5.) *Winter* (πρὸς δ' ἔτι καὶ χειμὼν ἦν, Xen. vi. 5. 50).

B.C.	OL.	
369.	102.4.	The terms of the peace. (Xen. vii. 1.) The proposal that Athens and Sparta should command by land and sea respectively is rejected; each city is to retain the entire command for five days, and then surrender it to the other for five days.
		Phlius.—When the Thebans were at Amyclae, the Phliasians, though abandoned, because last, by the general who was leading the detachment of auxiliaries from Prasiae, found their way to Sparta. They became allies of the Lacedaemonians, when they were most powerful, and remained faithful after Leuctra (ἀποστάντων μὲν πολλῶν περιοίκων ἀποστάντων δὲ πάντων τῶν Εἰλώτων, ἔτι δὲ τῶν συμμάχων, πλὴν πάνυ ὀλίγων, Xen. vii. 1. 22).
		When the Thebans entered the Peloponnesus, the Argives invaded Phlius (πανδημεί, Xen. viii. 2. 4). When they went away, the Phliasian horse attacked the rear of their army, and obtained some slight advantage. When the Thebans again entered, and the Arcadians and Eleans were going through Nemea to join them, Phliasian exiles offer to put Phlius in their power. The attempt is made, and fails; though the acropolis for a time is in the hands of the enemy. After harvest; for the sheaves which were in the acropolis were burnt to drive out the assailants (προσφέροντες τῶν δραγμάτων, ἃ ἔτυχον ἐξ αὐτῆς τῆς ἀκροπόλεως τεθερισμένα, Xen. vii. 2. 8).
		Summer. Second invasion of the Peloponnesus by the Thebans.
		They surprise the Lacedaemonian and Pellenians, who have guarded Oneum, and force their way through. They are joined by the Arcadians, Argives, and Eleans, and at once attack Sicyon, Pellene, etc.
		Dionysius of Syracuse sends help to the Spartans: 20 triremes with Celts and Iberians, and cavalry, which harass the Thebans in the plain before Corinth. The Thebans return home, failing to take Corinth; the contingent from Syracuse also returns.
		Lycomedes in Arcadia. He creates ill-feeling against the Thebans after their departure.

B.C.	OL.	
369.	102.4.	A man of position and birth, he claims Peloponnesus for the Arcadians as being autochthonous, urges them to take a leading part, and not to be at the beck and call of the Thebans. The Arcadians at once assist the Argives, who in an attack on Epidaurus are held in check by the Athenians under Chabrias, and the Corinthians. They also conquer the Lacedaemonian garrison at Asine. (Xen. vii. 1.)
368.		The Thebans march to Thessaly under Pelopidas to protect Larissa against Alexander of Pherae. He unites the Thessalian cities against Alexander, and brings the Macedonians into alliance with Thebes (taking 30 hostages, among them, Philip, the son of Amyntas, to Thebes).
		Attempt on the part of Ariobarzanes to bring about a peace, through Philiscus, at Delphi. The project falls to the ground, because the Thebans would not permit Messene to be subject to the Lacedaemonians. Philiscus gathers together a large force to support the Lacedaemonians, but nothing comes of it. (Xen. vii. 1.)
		Dionysius again sends help to the Lacedaemonians. They take Carya (putting the inhabitants to death), and invade the Parrhasians in Arcadia, when the auxiliaries wish to return to Syracuse, but, being cut off by the Argives and Arcadians, they send to the Lacedaemonians for help. The Arcadians are defeated with great slaughter. **The Tearless Victory.**
		Elis claims sovereignty over Lepreum and other towns in Triphylia, but these towns are admitted members of the Arcadian alliance, and the claims of Elis are rejected.
		The Arcadians and Argives again attack the Phliasians, but the Phliasian horse defeats them—$\epsilon\pi\grave{\iota}\ \tau\hat{\eta}\ \delta\iota\alpha\beta\acute{\alpha}\sigma\epsilon\iota\ \tau o\hat{\upsilon}\ \pi o\tau\alpha\mu o\hat{\upsilon}$—with the help of the Athenians.
		Dionysius again (cf. 383) attacks the Carthaginians, but he is defeated at Lilybaeum. He gains the prize for tragedy at the Lenaean festival, and soon after dies.
		Dionysius the younger succeeds his father $\sigma\chi\epsilon\delta\grave{o}\nu\ \pi\epsilon\rho\grave{\iota}\ \tau o\hat{\upsilon}\tau o\nu\ \tau\grave{o}\nu\ \chi\rho\acute{o}\nu o\nu$ (Xen. *Hell.* vii. 4. 12). He sends twelve triremes to the Lacedaemonians under Timocrates, who assists in taking Sellasia, and then departs.
		Plato in Sicily.

B.C.	OL.	
367.		**Third invasion of the Peloponnesus by the Thebans** under Epaminondas. He induces Peisius of Argos to secure the passes of Oneum, and then proceeds to Achaea. The Achaeans become allies of the Thebans (Epaminondas undertaking that the aristocracies shall not be banished, or the constitution changed), who return home. Great dissatisfaction at Thebes; Epaminondas is not re-elected commander; harmosts are sent to the Achaean cities; democracies established; the nobles banished, but the latter return and get possession of the cities. Euphron establishes himself at Sicyon by Arcadian (Theban) and Argive influence. **Embassy of the Greeks to Susa**; Pelopidas, Antiochus the Arcadian, Archidamus the Elean, Timagoras and Leon from Athens. Pelopidas proposes to the king, as the basis of a peace, that Messene is to be recognised as an independent city, and the Athenians are to draw up their ships. Leon resists on the part of the Athenians, and, on his return, Timagoras, who joined with Pelopidas, is put to death. The proposals lead to no result. Antiochus declares to the Arcadians, on his return, that the king's wealth is exaggerated, and the famous golden plane would not give shade to a lizard. (Xen. vii. 1. 38.) After the Thebans are in possession of Sicyon, an attempt is made to gain Phlius from thence, in which Euphron joins with 2000 mercenaries. The Pellenians join with them. The Phliasians are victorious over the Pellenians, and set up a trophy. (Xen. vii. 2. 11-15.) The Phliasians obtain supplies from Corinth. On one occasion, when Chares was with them as convoy, they persuade him to attack the Sicyonians in Thyamia. They reach them at sunset, disperse them, and take possession of their supplies. This was after the defeat of the Pellenians, who are now friends with Phlius (τοὺς ἀχρείους συνεκπέμψαι εἰς τὴν Πελλήνην. Xen. vii. 2. 18). (Grote, vii. 236 ff.)

B.C.	OL.	
367.		Xen. vii. 3—σχεδὸν δὲ περὶ τοῦτον τὸν χρόνον, Aeneas, the Arcadian general, is dissatisfied with affairs in Sicyon, and calls the bravest men in the city to his aid. Euphron retires to the harbour, which he offers to the Lacedaemonians through Pasimelus, the Corinthian.
Euphron is finally restored with the help of some Athenians (λαβὼν 'Αθήνηθεν ξενικόν), but the Theban harmost still retains the acropolis.
Euphron goes to Thebes to bribe the Thebans into giving up the acropolis to him. He is assassinated there by the opposite party. The assassins are acquitted (οἱ μέντοι πολῖται αὐτὸν, ὡς ἄνδρα ἀγαθὸν νομισάμενοι, ἔθαψάν τε ἐν τῇ ἀγορᾷ, καὶ ὡς ἀρχηγέτην τῆς πόλεως σέβονται. Xen. vii. 3. 12). (Grote, vii. 238.)
366.		**State congress at Thebes.** The states of Greece are summoned to Thebes to hear the king's letter, but they refuse to swear to the terms. Lycomedes will not recognise the superior position of Thebes, and retires, taking the Arcadian envoys with him. The Thebans then send round to the various cities to have the oaths taken, but Corinth refuses, and the whole project of a peace, under Persian influence and the leadership of Thebes, falls to the ground.
Pelopidas in Thessaly; he is seized and imprisoned by Alexander. The army which is sent out to recover him is defeated, and only saved by the skill of Epaminondas. A second expedition under Epaminondas is more successful. Pelopidas is set at liberty, but the influence of Thebes in Thessaly is greatly shaken. [The precise dates of these events are uncertain; Grote, vii. 250.] (Diod. xv. 71-75.)
Peloponnesus, ἔτι τειχιζόντων τῶν Φλιασίων τὴν Θυαμιάν καὶ τοῦ Χάρητος ἐτὶ παρόντος. Oropus is taken from Athens by exiles from Eretria, and in consequence Chares is ordered home. The harbour of the Sicyonians is now taken by the Arcadians and Theban party in the city. Oropus is put into the hands of the Thebans till the rival claims are decided (Xen. vii. 4. 1), for none of her allies assisted Athens.
Lycomedes, on the part of the Arcadians, negotiates a peace with Athens. On his return he perishes δαιμονιώτατα. Having entire liberty of choice he chose to disembark ἔνθα οἱ φυγάδες (his enemies) ἐτύγχανον ὄντες.

B.C.	OL.	
366.		The Athenians attempt to gain Corinth (Xen. vii. 4. 3), but the Corinthians send away all Athenians from their garrisons, and refuse to admit Chares with his fleet. They apply to Thebes for terms of peace, and after attempting to carry the Lacedaemonians with them, who refuse to renounce Messene, they and the Phliasians conclude peace with Thebes (ἐφ' ᾧ τε ἔχειν τὴν ἑαυτῶν ἑκάστους. Xen. vii. 4. 10).
		In spite of these terms the Argives retain Tricaranum, with the Phliasian exiles.
		The Eleans seize Lasion, which, formerly Elean, is now Arcadian. The Arcadians march against them and defeat them. They then proceed against the cities of the Acroreii, take all except Thraustus, and arrive at Olympia, where they establish themselves. [Differences in Elis; a democracy and an oligarchy. The democratical party think to make use of the presence of the Arcadians, and seize the acropolis, but they are dislodged and driven out. With the Arcadians the exiles occupy Pylus. The Arcadians seize Olourus, belonging to the Pellenians, which the Pellenians, who are now allies of the Lacedaemonians, recover.]
		Timotheus sent with a fleet to Asia to assist Ariobarzanes. He conquers Samos. Agesilaus also in Asia, but without an army.
365.		The Athenians admitted in part to the Chersonesus. Kleruchs are sent out both to Samos and to the Chersonesus.
		Timotheus acts against Cotys, king of Thrace; he supersedes Iphicrates, but fails to recover Amphipolis.
		The Thebans invade Thessaly, and Pelopidas is delivered.
	104.1.	The Arcadians again in Elis. The Eleans call upon the Lacedaemonians. Siege of Cromnus. The Lacedaemonians defeated, and Archidamus wounded. The Eleans recover Pylus.
364.		Pelopidas sent with an army against Alexander of Pherae. (Grote, vii. 271, etc.)
		The Arcadians at Olympia; they celebrate the festival, with the Pisatans. The Eleans attempt to prevent them, with great bravery.

B.C.	OL.	
363.	104.1.	**Thebes sends out a fleet under Epaminondas to the Hellespont and Bosporus.** **Pelopidas falls in battle against Alexander at Cynoscephalae.** The Thebans victorious. During the absence of Epaminondas, Orchomenus is destroyed by the Thebans. Arcadians at Olympia (Xen. vii. 4. 29). They use the sacred money (Xen. vii. 4. 33). The Mantineans refuse to do this; and the use is condemned in the Μύριοι; hence a quarrel between Arcadia and Mantinea, and a division between the Arcadians. The party who had availed themselves of the sacred money apply to Thebes; those who opposed it make peace with the Eleans. The peace party are arrested in great numbers at Tegea, but set at liberty on the representations of Mantinea.
362.		**Epaminondas marches into Peloponnese with all the Boeotians, the Euboeans, and many Thessalians.** In Peloponnese the Thebans had the Argives, Messenians, and part of the Arcadians; *i.e.* the Tegeatae, Megalopolitae, Aseatae, and Pallanteis. Epaminondas halts at Nemea, and from there passes to Tegea (εὐτυχῇ μὲν οὖν ἔγωγε οὐκ ἂν φήσαιμι τὴν στρατείαν αὐτῷ γενέσθαι· ὅσα μέντοι προνοίας ἔργα καὶ τόλμης ἐστὶν, οὐδέν μοι δοκεῖ ὁ ἀνὴρ ἐλλιπεῖν. Xen. vii. 5. 8). He narrowly escapes taking Sparta (*ib.* sect. 10). He returns to Tegea, and sends on his horse to Mantinea. (According to Xenophon, Epaminondas was repulsed at Sparta and his horse at Mantinea.) **Battle of Mantinea—Death of Epaminondas.** Indecisive result of the battle (νενικηκέναι δὲ φάσκοντες ἑκάτεροι οὔτε χώρᾳ, οὔτε πόλει, οὔτ᾽ ἀρχῇ οὐδέτεροι οὐδὲν πλέον ἔχοντες ἐφάνησαν ἢ πρὶν τὴν μάχην γενέσθαι· ἀκρισία δὲ καὶ ταραχὴ ἔτι πλείων μετὰ τὴν μάχην ἐγένετο ἢ πρόσθεν, ἐν τῇ Ἑλλάδι. Xen. vii. 5. 27).

B.C.	OL.	
362.	104.1.	Timotheus, who had been engaged making war upon Cotys and Amphipolis, is recalled by the Athenians; Ergophilus succeeds him, Callisthenes taking the command against Amphipolis. Alexander of Pherae equips a fleet, with which he captures Tenos, and afterwards defeats the Athenians at Peparethus, under Leosthenes. Encouraged by these successes, he makes a raid upon the Peiraeus and carries off much booty. Callisthenes fails to take Amphipolis, which is now under the protection of Philip of Macedon. Ergophilus also is unsuccessful against Cotys. Both are recalled and put on their trial.
	104.3.	Pammenes is sent into Peloponnesus, from Thebes, with 3000 men, to maintain the integrity of Megalopolis. (Diod. xv. 94. *See* Grote, vii. 315.) At this time Persia is in great disorder. Egypt has become an independent kingdom under Tachos, and Asia is in revolt. Datames, who has long been the mainstay of the imperial cause, now joins with Ariobarzanes, the satrap of the Hellespont, in the insurrection. Datames is assassinated, but the revolt is joined by Mausolus of Caria, Orontes of Mysia, and Autophradates of Lydia. Agesilaus and Chabrias join Tachos. Agesilaus, however, quickly abandons him for his rival Nectanebos, whom he establishes on the throne. Dion exiled from Syracuse by Dionysius II. *Aeschines, the orator, at Mantinea.*
361.	104.4.	Autocles is sent out from Athens to the Hellespont to secure the corn supplies. Miltocythes revolts from Cotys and sends to Athens for assistance, which is not granted to him. Autocles is recalled and put on his trial. Menon succeeds him in the command in Thrace, and, after a time, Timomachus succeeds Menon. Callistratus banished from Athens; Aristophon gains influence. Chares sails for Corcyra, but is too late to save the island for the Athenian alliance. Plato visits Dionysius II. for the second time.
360.		Cephisodotus succeeds Timomachus, who goes into exile to escape punishment. About this time Iphicrates retires from Thrace to Lesbos. Charidemus, who returns from Asia, supports Cotys, who now seizes Sestus, and claims the Chersonese.

B.C.	OL.	
360.	105.1.	Assassination of Cotys; he is succeeded by his son Cersobleptes (who also has the support of Charidemus); the two compel Cephisodotus to conclude a disgraceful treaty, in which Cardia is ceded to Charidemus. About this time the revolt in Persia is crushed.
359.		The claims of Cersobleptes to Thrace are opposed by two rivals, Berisades and Amadocus. Charidemus stations himself at Cardia; Miltocythes falls into his hands; he delivers him over to the Cardians, who put him to death, together with his son. Indignation at this act enables Berisades and Amadocus to increase their power. Thrace is divided into three equal portions; the Chersonese is to be given up to Athens, but there is great delay in ceding it.
	105.2.	Death of Artaxerxes II., king of Persia, and accession of Ochus. **Assassination of Alexander of Pherae.** By the connivance of his wife, he was murdered by her three brothers Tisiphonus, Peitholaus, and Lycophron. (Cf. Grote, vii. 638.) Perdiccas of Macedon slain in battle against the Illyrians. **Accession of Philip II.** He conciliates the Athenians by withdrawing from Amphipolis and offering peace, which is accepted. He obtains a victory over the Paeonians and Illyrians. Chabrias now returns from Egypt to Athens.
358.		The Chersonese is finally handed over to Athens. Great extent of the Athenian power at this time. Euboea, which, since the battle of Leuctra (371 B.C.) has been under Theban control, now revolts. Athens sends prompt aid under Timotheus, and rescues the island. First instance of voluntary trierarchs.
	105.3.	
		Revolt of the Allies from Athens. SOCIAL WAR, 358-356. Chios, Cos, Rhodes, and Byzantium revolt from Athens. They are supported by Mausolus of Caria. Battle of Chios; defeat of the Athenians, and death of Chabrias.

B.C.	OL.	
358.	105.3.	Philip besieges Amphipolis, and prevents the city from applying for aid to Athens.
357.		Chares, Timotheus, and Iphicrates in the Hellespont with a fleet to act against the allies. Chares, against the wish of his colleagues, attacks the enemy, and is unsuccessful. On his return to Athens he impeaches them. Iphicrates is acquitted; Timotheus is condemned to a fine of 100 talents. He retires to Chalcis.
	105.4.	Philip conquers Amphipolis. The Olynthians, alarmed at the fall of the city, offer alliance to Athens, which is rejected. Philip, though an ally of Athens, makes himself master of Pydna and Potidaea, towns belonging to Athens, and gives Potidaea to the Olynthians. **War between Athens and Philip (357-346).** Return of Dion to Syracuse. Death of Agesilaus on his return from Egypt. He is succeeded by his son Archidamus (357-338). [Others put his death in 361.]
356.		Chares, at the head of a large Athenian fleet, enters the service of Artabazus, then in revolt against the king; with his help, Artabazus gains a great victory over Tithraustes. The king supports the revolted allies, so that Athens, in alarm, comes to terms with them.
	103.1.	Foundation of Philippi. Philip, now in possession of the mines of Pangaeum, issues a gold coinage. Defeat of the Illyrians under Parmenio. **Birth of Alexander the Great, son of Philip and Olympias, the daughter of the King of the Molossians.** Dissensions between Heraclides and Dion, who retires to Leontini.
355		**Outbreak of the Phocian or Third Sacred War.**

B.C.	OL.	
355.	106.1.	The Phocians are accused of occupying some of the sacred land belonging to the temple at Delphi. A fine is imposed upon them by the Amphictyonic Council. The Phocians, led by Philomelus, refuse to pay the fine. They seize Delphi, from which the Locrians are unable to dislodge them. An extraordinary Amphictyonic Council is summoned, and war declared against them. Philomelus attempts to gain support throughout Greece.
	106 2.	
		Mausolus of Caria establishes an oligarchical form of government in Chios, Cos, and Rhodes.
		Demosthenes "Against Androtion."
354.		The Thebans march out to Delphi against the Phocians. Philomelus is defeated and slain, but the war is continued by Onomarchus and Phayllus. Free use is made of the sacred treasures of the temple to attract mercenaries from all quarters.
		Eubulus minister of finance at Athens. Death of Timotheus at Chalcis.
	106 3.	*Demosthenes "Against Leptines," and "On the Symmories."*
		The first oration was a reply to a proposal to cancel all immunities, or exemptions from public service, except those granted to the descendants of Harmodius and Aristogiton. The second was intended partly to soothe the agitation for war with Persia by showing how impossible it was for Athens to contend with the great king, and partly to sketch a new system of trierarchical service and taxation.
353.		Onomarchus enters into a league with Lycophron and Peitholaus, the tyrants of Pherae. This renders him secure on the side of Thessaly. He also obtains some successes in Boeotia. Philip appears in Thessaly; he is victorious over Phayllus, but so severely defeated by Onomarchus in two engagements, that he is compelled to leave for Thessaly.

B.C.	OL.	
353.	106.4.	Pammenes, the Theban, marches to support Artabazus, in revolt against the king. He is accompanied along the coast by Philip. Philip takes Abdera, Maronea, and also Methone. Chares conquers Sestos. Dion is assassinated at Syracuse by Callippus.
352.		Onomarchus conquers Coronea, but, being summoned again into Thessaly to aid the tyrants of Pherae against Philip, he is utterly defeated and slain on the coast of Magnesia. Philip takes Pherae and Pagasae, and occupies Magnesia, but is prevented from going further by the Athenians, who occupy Thermopylae in force. Phayllus continues the war; the treasures of Delphi enable him, even yet, to attract followers by the prospect of high pay. He invades eastern Locris, and there
	107.1.	falls; his nephew Phalaecus succeeds him. Peace concluded between Athens and Olynthus. Philip returns from Thessaly to Thrace; leagues himself with Cardia, Byzantium, and Perinthus. Cersobleptes is compelled to accept terms of peace. Philip falls sick and retires from Thrace. *Speeches of Demosthenes " For the Megalopolitans," "Against Timocrates," and "Against Aristocrates."* The Spartans, thinking the Thebans too weak to interfere in the Peloponnesus, are anxious to break up the city of Megalopolis. Envoys from Sparta and Megalopolis appear at Athens. Demosthenes supports the cause of Megalopolis, but in vain. But owing to the defeat of Onomarchus, the Thebans are able to invade Peloponnesus (for the last time) and protect the city.—Timocrates had proposed a measure that all debtors to the state should be allowed to give security for their debts to the end of the year. The law had been hastily and informally passed, and was rescinded as illegal. —Aristocrates had brought forward a measure that any one who attacked the life of Charidemus should be an outlaw in Athenian dominions. This Demosthenes opposed, with what result is not known.

B.C.	OL.	
351.	107.1.	Death of Mausolus of Caria; accession of Artemisia. Philip attacks Arybbas, king of the Molossi, his wife's father.
	107.2.	*Demosthenes' "For the Rhodians," and "First Philippic."* The Rhodians took advantage of the death of Mausolus to apply to Athens for help in ridding themselves of the Carian mercenaries who maintained the authority of Mausolus in the island. Demosthenes pleads their cause, but without result.—In the "First Philippic" Demosthenes calls attention to the dangerous advances which Philip has made, and the unsatisfactory nature of the war, which has now lingered on since 357 B.C. If results are to be hoped for, war must be organised with energy. Plutarch of Eretria applies for assistance to Athens to enable him to maintain his position.
350.		The Athenians under Phocion in Euboea. Battle of Tamynae, and narrow escape of the Athenians. Phocion returns to Athens, but Zaretra falls into the hands of the enemy.
	107.3	Apollodorus proposes that the surplus funds of the state should be used for purposes of war. His proposition is rejected as illegal, and it is forbidden, under pain of death, to apply in paying the soldiers the money which has been used for theatrical exhibitions. (Cf. 338 B.C.) Demosthenes and Midias. Midias assaulted Demosthenes when choregus; for this, legal proceedings were taken against him, but the matter is allowed to drop. (The speech "Against Midias" was never delivered, and was probably written in 349 B.C.) The incident shows the height to which party spirit had run at Athens, and the hatred Demosthenes had brought upon himself for exposing the feeble war policy of Eubulus.
349.		**War between Philip and Olynthus.**

B.C.	OL.	
349.	107.3.	In 357 B.C. Olynthus, alarmed at the fall of Amphipolis, wished to enter into negotiations with Athens, but was prevented by Philip. In 352, when Philip was in Thessaly, Athens and Olynthus concluded a peace, and again, in 350, Olynthus requested troops from Athens to maintain her frontier. Philip, now, having completed his preparations, calls on the Olynthians to surrender his two step-brothers.
	107.4.	The Olynthians understand this to be equivalent to a declaration of war, and appear at Athens, asking for assistance. An alliance is concluded with the Olynthians; and Chares sent to their assistance with 2000 mercenaries and 30 triremes. "*Olynthiac Orations*" *of Demosthenes;* in which he endeavours (1) to point out the importance of the crisis; (2) to rouse the Athenians to *personal* service; (3) to exhibit the weakness of Philip's position; (4) to induce the Athenians to apply the surplus revenues to military purposes. The order of the orations is doubtful.
348.		**Fall of Olynthus.** For a time Philip had been engaged putting down a rising in Thessaly. Now he returns in person to Chalcidice and begins to press the cities hard; some are taken, some receive him. The Olynthians send twice to Athens for help; but the Athenians defer real assistance till too late. Olynthus and thirty-two confederate cities are destroyed, the inhabitants being sold into slavery. Philip celebrates Olympic games in Macedonia. Attempt to unite the Greeks against Philip. Aeschines in Peloponnesus. The attempt fails.
	108.1.	
347.		Negotiations for peace between Athens and Philip. These were at first informal, carried on by private persons who had access to Philip. They

B.C.	OL.	
347.	108.1.	were assisted by the conduct of the Phocians, who refused to allow the Athenians to enter the pass of Thermopylae. Finally, Philocrates proposes (Eubulus supporting him) that ten ambassadors be sent to Philip to treat.
	108.2.	The Thebans request Philip's aid against the Phocians, who are still commanded by Phalaecus. The Phocians send for assistance to Athens, which is immediately granted, but when the Athenian forces arrive, Phalaecus, who holds the pass of Thermopylae, refuses to admit them.
347-323.		Ten talents are raised annually by a property tax for the fleet, etc., at Athens.
346.		**The Peace of Philocrates. Destruction of the Phocians, and end of the Sacred War.**
		The envoys return from Philip to Athens with a letter. He demands that Halus and the Phocians shall be excluded from the list of Athenian allies. The question debated on 18th and 19th Elaphebolion. Demosthenes opposes it. But the Macedonian envoys refuse to ratify the peace without the disputed clause. Aeschines induces the Athenians to give way; the oaths are taken at Athens; an embassy is despatched to take the oaths from Philip and his allies. Great delay. Philip takes the oaths at Pella; his allies at Pherae. The embassy returns to Athens on Scirophorion 13th, when Philip is close upon Thermopylae. Demosthenes urges that a force be sent to the pass. Aeschines soothes all apprehension and has a decree passed that the Phocians be renounced as allies if they refuse to give up the temple. Phalaecus makes his terms with Philip, who thus becomes master of the pass and Phocis.
	108.3.	The Amphictyonic Council decrees the destruction of Phocis as a Grecian State.
		Philip chosen to preside over the Pythian games.
		Demosthenes, "*On the Peace,*" urges the Athenians to acquiesce in the peace now that it is made; the conduct of the Amphictyonic Council in giving up Phocis to Philip for destruction was not worth a contest when so much had been abandoned.

B.C.	OL.	
345.	108.3.	Return of Dionysius II. to Syracuse.
		Great prosperity of Athens at this time. New dockhouses are erected in the Peiraeus under the superintendence of Philon, and the fleet raised to 300 triremes (Dem. *De fals. leg.* p. 369).
		On the proposal of Demophilus the list of citizens is revised and large numbers (5000 or more) are struck off the roll.
		New arrangements appear to have been made in the management of the assembly. Hitherto at meetings nine proedri had presided, chosen by lot, by the chairman of the prytanies from the nine tribes, excluding his own. From these the chairman of the assembly was chosen. Now a "presiding tribe" was added to the proedri and prytanies, which gathered round the bema, and if necessary kept order.
	108.4.	*Aeschines "Against Timarchus."* After the embassy to take the oaths (346), Demosthenes had indicted Aeschines for misconduct, Timarchus supporting the indictment. Aeschines, to gain time, attacks Timarchus for his scandalous life. Timarchus loses all civil rights.
		Philip attacks the Illyrians, Dardanians, and Triballi. Negotiations about the Chersonese and Thracian towns still go on between Athens and Philip.
		The orators Lycurgus and Hyperides form a strong anti-Macedonian party with Demosthenes. They are joined by Diotimus, Nausicles, Polyeuctus, and others. Eubulus and Phocion desire peace at any price. Aeschines, Demades, and Philocrates head the Macedonian party.
344.		Philip establishes oligarchical government in Thessaly by means of a decarchy. Then he passes into Peloponnesus to assist Argos and Messene against Sparta. The Athenians interfere. Demosthenes himself visits both cities and urges them against friendship with Philip. Philip sends ambassadors to the Athenians to complain.

B.C.	OL.	
344.	109.1.	*"Second Philippic"* of Demosthenes, in which he proposes a reply to Philip, a written document, which has not come down to us, and shows the real relations of Philip to Athens.
		Timoleon leaves Corinth for Syracuse and, in a short time, Dionysius agrees to quit Ortygia; he is brought to Corinth.
343.		Hyperides attacks Philocrates for his conduct in regard to Macedon; Philocrates goes into exile, and in his absence is condemned to death.
		The remnant of the mercenaries of Phalaecus, who perished in an attempt to take Cydonia in Crete, take service with some Elean exiles, whom they assist to return home. The attempt is unsuccessful. The mercenaries who are taken captive are partly sold and partly massacred (Diod. xvi. 61-63).
		Philip makes an attempt upon Megara, which fails. Megara enters into alliance with Athens. Nisaea is fortified and the long walls restored.
		The Delians attempt to set aside the claim of the Athenians to the temple of Apollo in the island. The question referred to the Amphictyonic Council. Aeschines, who had been chosen to represent Athens, is set aside, and Hyperides is sent in his place. The Athenians maintain their claim. (*Spring.*)
	109.2.	Philip sends Python to Athens to attack the anti-Macedonian party. In return Hegesippus is sent to Philip to demand the restitution of Halonnesus, and the Thracian towns, and to fix the limits of the Chersonese. Philip receives him with marked discourtesy. (*Summer.*)
		The case of misconduct in the Legation (346). Demosthenes and Aeschines. Aeschines is acquitted by a small majority (thirty votes).
		Philip in Euboea. He establishes his power there by means of tyrants—Clitarchus at Eretria.

B.C.	OL.	
343.	109.2.	*Antiphanes, comic poet. Period of Middle Comedy.*
		Winter. Philip in Epirus, where he establishes Alexander on the throne in the room of his uncle Arybbas. From Epirus he marches on Ambracia, and threatens Acarnania and Leucas, but without effect, for the Athenians rouse the Peloponnesians to a sense of the danger (Demosthenes, Polyeuctus, and Hegesippus sent as ambassadors) and also send forces to Acarnania to support Arybbas, who is hospitably received at Athens.
342.		Philip returns home through Thessaly, where he establishes tetrarchies, under his own control.
		He resumes negotiations with Athens. His letter, and the speech of Hegesippus ("*De Halonneso*").
		He makes an expedition into Thrace.
	109.3.	In Euboea his troops take Oreus, and establish Philistides there as tyrant. Alliance between Chalcis and Athens.
		Diopithes in the Hellespont. New settlers are sent from Athens to the Chersonese about this time or a little earlier.
		Aristotle summoned to the Macedonian court.
341.		Philip in Thrace.
		Difficulties arise in the Chersonese between the Attic cleruchs and the Cardians. Diopithes advances into Thrace to aid Philip's enemies; Philip addresses a letter of remonstrance to Athens.
		Demosthenes' "*De Chersoneso*" and "*Third Philippic.*" In the "De Chersoneso" he urges that Philip, though nominally at peace, is really at war, so that it would be foolish to recall or
	109.4	punish Diopithes. A great danger is impending, against which every precaution should be taken. The "Third Philippic" is to the same effect, but with less special reference to the Chersonese. Athens must arm if the freedom of Hellas is to be secured.

B.C.	OL.	
341.	109.4.	Attempts are made to establish a league against Philip. Demosthenes goes to Byzantium, Hyperides to Chios and Rhodes. Alliance between Byzantium and Athens.
		Oreus is liberated by the combined efforts of the Athenians, Chalcidians, and Megarians.
340.		Philip in Thrace.
		Embassies sent from Athens to Peloponnesus, and arrangements made for the league against Philip. The league to include Euboea, Acarnania, Corinth, Achaea, Corcyra, Megara.
		Eretria liberated by the Athenians under Phocion. Philip marches upon the Chersonese. He besieges Perinthus, and, failing to take it, invests Byzantium.
	110.1.	**War declared upon Philip by the Athenians.**
		Reform of the trierarchic system by Demosthenes. The companies done away with, and rates levied according to property. ("*De Corona*," 260 *f.*)
		The Byzantines supported by the Athenians and the allies.
		Ochus reduces Egypt to submission.
		Great defeat of the Carthaginians in Sicily on the Crimesus by Timoleon.
339.		Aeschines at the Amphictyonic assembly with Midias. He accuses the Amphissean Locrians of sacrilege. **Amphictyonic War.**
		Philip raises the siege of Byzantium and marches into Scythia to avenge himself upon Atheas, who, after seeking his assistance, had rejected it. On his return he is attacked by the
	110.2.	Triballi, and severely wounded. Subsequently he is chosen to lead the Amphictyons in their attack on Amphissa. He defeats the Amphisseans and destroys their city. Then he passes into Phocis, and takes possession of Elatea.
		Preparations for war at Athens.

B.C.	OL.	
338.	110.2.	Demosthenes crowned (at the Dionysia, *April*). The "theoric fund" applied to military purposes. Negotiations between Athens and Thebes. Lycurgus minister of finance at Athens. Demosthenes crowned again (at the Panathenaea).
	110.3.	**Battle of Chaeronea.** Victory of Philip. (*September*.) Measures for the defence of Athens: the walls repaired under the care of Demosthenes. Phocion assumes the military command. The Thebans capitulate and are severely treated; the Cadmea is occupied by a Macedonian garrison. Orchomenus, Plataea, and Thespiae restored. **The Peace of Demades** between Athens and Philip. Athens surrenders her possessions except Lemnos, Imbros, and Samos; the tribute, and the hegemony. She receives Oropus. Philip marches by Megara and Corinth into the Peloponnesus. In a synod at Corinth, he arranges the affairs of Hellas; is chosen general of the Hellenic forces against Persia. *Death of Isocrates.*
337.		Marriage of Philip and Cleopatra.
	110.4.	Preparations for the invasion of Persia; Pixodarus of Caria enters into an alliance with Philip. Death of Timoleon at Syracuse.
336.		Improvement of the fortifications of Athens, in which Demosthenes takes a leading part. Proposal of Ctesiphon to crown Demosthenes at the great Dionysia. Aeschines opposes. **Assassination of Philip at the marriage of his daughter Cleopatra.** (*July.*) Accession of
	111.1.	Alexander. He marches into Greece, where he is accepted by the Amphictyonic Council and by Athens. At Corinth, he is appointed leader of the Greeks against the Persians. The Hellenic cities are to be free, and autonomous; no despot is to be established or

B.C.	OL.	
336.	111.1.	restored; navigation is to be free and unimpeded. These terms the Macedonians do not strictly observe. Accession of Darius Codomannus. [Ochus had been assassinated two years before by Bagoas, who raised Arses, the youngest son of Ochus, to the throne, but murdered him in the third year of his reign. He then chose Codomannus, who took the name of Darius.]
335.		Alexander in Thrace and Illyria. **Revolt of Thebes.** The Thebans, taking advantage of the absence of Alexander, return from exile at Athens, instigate the people, and besiege the Macedonians in the Cadmea.
	111.2.	Alexander at once marches upon Thebes and besieges the city, which is soon captured. All the inhabitants are massacred, and the walls razed to the ground. Alexander demands the surrender of the leaders of the anti-Macedonian party at Athens :—Demosthenes, Lycurgus, Polyeuctus, Moerocles, Ephialtes, Damon, Callisthenes, and Charidemus. He is prevailed on to accept the banishment of Charidemus and Ephialtes, and omit the rest. He returns to Pella. [The authorities for the history of Alexander are Arrian's *Anabasis*, Curtius, and Justinus.]
334.		Alexander passes into Persia. **Battle of the Granicus,** and defeat of the Persians under Spithridates, satrap of Lydia, Arsites, viceroy of Phrygia, and Memnon. Asia Minor on this side of Taurus falls into the hands of Alexander. Sardis receives
	111.3.	him. Ephesus is divided by faction; for a time Memnon, on his retreat from the Granicus, organises an opposition to Alexander, but, when he approaches, Memnon retires to Halicarnassus. Democracy is established; the revenues are given to the temple of Artemis, and the right of asylum is extended over a stadium in every direction.

B.C.	OL.	
334.	111.3.	Tralles and Magnesia on the Maeander offer submission. Parmenio is sent to occupy them. Democracies are established everywhere in the Greek cities. Smyrna is rebuilt.
Alexander at Miletus, which adheres to the Persian cause owing to the proximity of the fleet. The town is taken by storm. The Grecian fleet being no match for the Persian, is disbanded. From Miletus, Alexander passes to Caria. Ada, the deposed queen, and the Greek cities join him, but Halicarnassus, the centre of Persian influence, resists, under the command of Memnon. After a stubborn resistance, the city is set on fire and abandoned. Alexander takes possession, and breaks it up into six hamlets.
Towards winter, Alexander sends some troops home, and with the remainder winters in Lycia, at Phaselis. The Lycians retain their old constitution, a confederacy of twenty-three cities.
333.		Alexander in Pisidia, from whence he marches to Celaenae in Phrygia, and to Gordium. The Persian fleet achieves success in the Aegean, gaining Chios and Lesbos. Death of Memnon, the commander during the siege of Mitylene.
Memnon's plan for acting on the defensive at Mt. Amanus is abandoned by Darius; execution of Charidemus, the Athenian, who openly opposes offensive operations. The Greek mercenaries serving in the Persian fleet are recalled to join the army.
	111.4.	Alexander marches from Gordium through Paphlagonia and Cappadocia to the Taurus, which he is allowed to pass without opposition. He enters Tarsus, and falls ill. On his recovery he marches through Issus to Myriandrus, when he finds that Darius has crossed Mount Amanus to Issus. He returns.

B.C.	OL.	
333.	111.4.	**Battle of Issus.** Defeat and flight of Darius. Capture of the royal Persian women.
		Capture of Damascus with large treasure, and submission of Phoenicia, except Tyre and Gaza.
		Darius offers terms of peace, which are rejected.
		The success at Issus crushed anti-Macedonian efforts in Greece. Yet Agis, king of Lacedaemon, obtains money from the Persian fleet, and makes himself master of Crete, which, however, he is unable to hold for more than two years.
332.		**Siege of Tyre.**
		The Cyprian ships join Alexander, and the greater part of the Phoenician: being now master of an efficient fleet, he is able to
	112.1.	blockade Tyre by sea as well as land. After a siege of seven months the city is captured by storm.
		Darius again offers peace, but his overtures are rejected.
		Recovery of the Aegean by Alexander's fleet, which is now superior to the Persian.
		Siege of Gaza, which after two months is taken by storm. Cruel treatment of Batis, the commander of Gaza. Alexander in Egypt, where he **founds Alexandria**, and visits the temple of Ammon, claiming to be the son of Zeus.
331.		The result of the successes of Alexander had been to restore to the Greek cities and islands a large measure of independence. The despots of the island cities are now brought to him in Egypt; he hands them over to their citizens, who, in most cases, put them to death.
		Alexander marches through Phoenicia to Thapsacus on the Euphrates; crosses Mesopotamia, and fords the Tigris. He finds Darius at Gaugamela, thirty miles west of Arbela.

B.C.	OL.	
331.	112.2.	**Battle of Arbela.** Defeat and flight of Darius; overthrow of the Persian empire. Alexander proceeds to Babylon, from thence to Susa, and after passing the "Susian Gates" to Persepolis, where he finds the royal treasures.
330.		He pursues Darius to Ecbatana, from whence he sends home the Thessalian cavalry. Then he follows Darius to the "Caspian Gates." Conspiracy against Darius, headed by Bessus: in spite of the efforts of Alexander to overtake and secure him, Darius is slain. Alexander at Hecatompylus: after resting there he subdues Hyrcania, and from thence passes
	112.3.	into Asia and Drangiana. Execution of Parmenio and his son Philotas, on account of their supposed complicity in conspiracy. Antipater, Alexander's general in command, being compelled to suppress a rising in Thrace, withdraws troops from Greece. Agis heads a revolt in Peloponnesus, but he is quickly crushed by Antipater on his return, and slain. "**Case of the Crown**" at Athens. Aeschines had indicted Ctesiphon for proposing that Demosthenes should be crowned at the "Tragedies" (Great Dionysia) in 336. The case is now brought on. Aeschines, failing to obtain one-fifth of the votes, is fined 1000 drachmae, and leaves Athens.
329.		Alexander crosses the Paropamisus (Hindoo-Koosh) into Bactria, thence he passes, across the Oxus, into Sogdiana. He captures Bessus, and massacres the Branchidae, in return for the treachery of their ancestors in the time
	112.4.	of Xerxes. He proceeds to the Jaxartes, the extreme northward limit of his marches. Foundation of Alexandria ad Jaxartem. Returning, he crosses the Oxus to Zariaspa, where he puts Bessus to death.

B.C.	OL.	
328.	112.4.	Alexander at Marakanda (Samarcand). Further subjugation of Sogdiana. Murder of Cleitus.
327.	113.1.	Complete subjugation of Sogdiana. Alexander proceeds to Bactra, where he marries Roxana, daughter of the Bactrian chief, Oxyartes. He demands divine honours, which are opposed by Callisthenes. In consequence,
	113.2.	Callisthenes is shortly afterwards put to death. Alexander crosses the Paropamisus into India. Conquest of the country between the Paropamisus and the Indus.
326.	113.3.	Alexander crosses the Indus, and proceeds to the Hydaspes (Jelum). **Battle with Porus**, at the crossing of the river. Porus defeated, but honourably treated by Alexander. He pushes his conquests to the **Hyphasis (Sutlej)**, **where his army refuses to advance further.**
325.		Returning to the Hydaspes, he sails down that river and the Indus to the Indian Ocean, the army marching alongside. On reaching the sea, Nearchus conducts the fleet from the
	113.4.	Indus to the Tigris, while Alexander marches through Gedrosia to Carmania, and from thence to Persepolis.
324.		Alexander continues his march to Susa, where the fleet joins his army. He examines into the conduct of the satraps during his absence,
	114.1.	and punishes some. Flight of Harpalus, the satrap of Babylon, to Greece, with a large treasure.
		Alexander urges intermarriage between his Macedonian soldiers and Persian women, which causes great discontent. A number of Asiatic soldiers are hired and trained for service in the army. Hence a mutiny arises among the Macedonian soldiers, part of whom are disbanded and sent home under Craterus. Alexander also prepares to enlarge his fleet. Death of Hephaestion.

B.C.	OL.	
324.	114.1.	Harpalus comes to Athens after his flight from Babylon. The Athenians refuse to accept his offers; but will not surrender him to Antipater. They sequestrate his treasure for Alexander. Harpalus escapes arrest by flight. Demosthenes is accused of appropriating part of the money of Harpalus, the sum counted being less than the amount given out by Harpalus. Demosthenes condemned and fined fifty talents. He leaves Athens.
323.		**Alexander marches to Babylon, and prepares for the conquest of Arabia. His illness and death** (aged thirty-two years and eight months).
	114.2.	Athens, on the news of Alexander's death, claims to liberate the Greeks, and invites co-operation. Demosthenes is recalled. Leosthenes, with the confederate forces (in which Sparta and Boeotia are not included) marches to Thessaly. **Lamian War.** He is victorious over Antipater, whom he drives into Lamia. But soon after Leosthenes is slain, and succeeded by Antiphilus. Antipater escapes.
322.	114.3.	Antipater is joined by Craterus with a large army. **Battle of Crannon.** End of the war. The confederation breaks up. Antipater advances to Thebes. Athens submits. She agrees to pay the whole expense of the war, to surrender Demosthenes and Hyperides, to receive a Macedonian garrison into Munychia, and disfranchise the poorer citizens (12,000 of whom are deported).
		Death of Demosthenes at Calauria. He poisons himself to escape arrest by the soldiers of Antipater, who has already put Hyperides to death.
		Death of Aristotle.

PART III.

THE CONSTITUTIONAL HISTORY OF ATHENS AND LACEDAEMON.

CONSTITUTION OF ATHENS.

The Population of Attica.

The Athenians claimed to be "autochthonous," *i.e.* to have inhabited Attica from the beginning, undisturbed by foreign conquest and admixture, but it is very doubtful whether this claim can be admitted. It would rather appear that in early times the population of the country was composed of various elements, Phoenicians (at Marathon and Melite), Carians (at Athens), and even Thracians (at Eleusis), who were partly expelled and partly absorbed by Pelasgian and Ionian tribes.

Early Forms of Combination.

We are told that Cecrops, the first king of the country, united the various villages of Attica into twelve townships or πόλεις. This legend is so far true that in Attica, as elsewhere in Greece, the villages or hamlets, which were in the first instance unprotected by walls, and at a distance from the seaboard, tended to unite into larger or smaller aggregates. The more powerful settlements compelled the less powerful in their immediate neighbourhood to join them (as Aphidna), while others combined for purposes of religious worship. Of such combinations in Attica we have instances in the Tetrapolis, a union of the four towns Marathon, Oenoe, Probalinthus, and Trikorythus, the Tetrakomi, and the Trikomi.

The Union of Attica.

The first event of importance in the constitutional history of Attica is the *union of the whole country* round Athens as a centre (συνοικισμός). This is said to have been the work of *Theseus*, who either persuaded or compelled the separate towns to give up their independence, and made Athens the ruling city. As Theseus is regarded in legend as a foreigner, we may perhaps conclude that this union was brought about by foreign conquest. The union was commemorated. by the festival of the *Synoecia*.

The Tribes.

With this union of the whole of Attica is sometimes connected the establishment of the four tribes, the *Geleontes, Hopletes, Argades,* and *Aegicoreis,* into which the whole population was divided. These tribes were again divided into twelve phratries (three in each tribe), each of which contained thirty families (γένη). The precise nature of this arrangement is disputed. The difficulties cannot be satisfactorily removed, but it seems reasonable to conclude:

(1) That the tribes did not denote occupations in Attica.
(2) That they did not mark local divisions of the country.

In all probability they were very ancient divisions of the Ionic people, which were introduced into Attica when the country was united under Ionic influence. And as it was impossible in early times to classify the nation on any other basis but that of supposed gentile and tribal connection, this division, with the development of phratries and gentes, was adopted in order to bring the population of Attica into some kind of arrangement.

Classes.

Another division of the population separated them into *Eupatrids, Geomori,* and *Demiurgi,* of whom the first were the nobility, the second the yeomen and farmers (who farmed their own land, or that of the Eupatrids), the third the artisans or labourers. Though the tribes included all these classes, the administration and government of the tribes, phratries, and families were in the hands of the Eupatrids. The leaders of the tribes were known as Phylobasileis. The Geomori and Demiurgi can have had nothing more than a very subordinate place in the political constitution.

The Monarchy.

From the earliest times Attica was governed by kings. But about the date of the Dorian migration into the Peloponnesus an important change took place in the succession. *Exiles from Pylus*, who had fled to Attica for refuge, attained to the throne by their bravery and devotion in defending the country from invasion.

In the reign of Melanthus, the first of these Pylian kings, the festival of the *Apaturia* is said to have been introduced. As participation in this festival is a special mark of Ionian descent, we may suppose that Attica was by this time entirely under Ionian influence. The self-sacrifice of Codrus, the son of Melanthus, who by his death delivered Athens from the attack of the Dorians, secured for his family the possession of the throne. They were known as the *Medontidae* from Medon, the son and successor of Codrus.

Modification of the Royal Power.

It seems that from the accession of the Medontidae the royal power underwent a series of modifications. In the first place the kings became *archons*, to some extent responsible to or dependent on the order of the Eupatrids. Then in the year 752 the archonship was no longer tenable for life, but for *ten years* only,[1] and in 712 it was opened to all

---

[1] Paus. iv. 5, 10. 'Αθήνησι δὲ οὐκ ἦσάν πω τότε (Ol. 9. 2.) οἱ τῷ κλήρῳ κατ' ἐνιαυτὸν ἄρχοντες. τοὺς γὰρ ἀπὸ Μελάνθου, καλουμένους δὲ Μεδοντίδας, κατ' ἀρχὰς μὲν ἀφείλοντο ὁ δῆμος τῆς ἐξουσίας τὸ πολύ, καὶ ἀντὶ βασιλείας μετέστησαν ἐς ἀρχὴν ὑπεύθυνον, ὕστερον δὲ καὶ προθεσμίαν ἐτῶν δέκα ἐποίησαν αὐτοῖς τῆς ἀρχῆς.

the *Eupatrids*. Finally in 683 the decennial archons were abolished, and in their place were chosen *nine annual archons*. Of these the first was known as the *Archon*, the second as the *Basileus*, in which capacity he discharged the religious functions of the earlier kings, and the third as the *Polemarch*, or leader of the army. The remaining six were *Thesmothetae* or law-givers, *i.e.* they were occupied with the law. These officers formed a board, with a special place of meeting, the Prytaneum, in which they were allowed maintenance at the public cost. The collection of the sums necessary for their maintenance was perhaps managed by the *Colacretae*, who were thus the earliest financial officers at Athens.

The Naucraries.

This meagre record is all that we really know of the constitutional changes at Athens down to the times of Draco, who in 620 B.C. was commissioned to write down the laws of Athens. But we may venture to assume that there was at Athens a council of the Eupatrids, for without this it is difficult to see what is meant by the responsibility of the archon. Out of this council in later times the Senate of the Areopagus may have been formed. From the fact that even in the seventh century B.C., Athens engaged in war with Megara for the possession of Salamis, it is probable that at an early time arrangements had been made for the maintenance of a fleet. For this purpose, the whole country was divided into forty-eight sections called *Naucraries*, each of which was called upon to provide a ship. The Naucraries were united into *Trittyes*, of which there were twelve ; of the Trittyes three were allotted to each tribe. As the burden which fell upon each Naucraria was equal, we may presume that the tribes by this time at least represented a tolerably equal division of the inhabitants in point of wealth. In each Naucraria there was a president or prytaneus. These officers, forty-eight in number, formed a board in addition to the nine archons. It is also supposed that each Naucraria, in addition to a ship, furnished two horsemen for the service of the state. If this be true, the navy of Athens before the time of Solon amounted to forty-eight vessels, and the cavalry to ninety-six mounted soldiers.

The Laws of Draco.

Towards the end of the seventh century factions began to arise at Athens. The inhabitants of the plains (*Pedieis*), who were the rich land-owners, the mountaineers (*Diacrii*), who were poorer, and lived by their herds and flock and the men of the shore (*Paralii*), appear as three parties at variance with each other. An obscure and mutilated inscription[1] seems to indicate that the nobility felt themselves unable to resist the pressure brought to bear upon them by the tillers of the soil, so that for a time four archons only were chosen by the Eupatrids, three by those who lived away from Athens in the country, and two by the Demiurgi. Archons so elected are said to have held office in the year after Damasias (*i.e.* in 638 B.C.). But whatever the concession was, it was quickly cancelled. The constitution remained as before, till the beginning of a change was brought about by the publication of the *Laws of Draco* in 621 B.C.

Of these laws we know that they were regarded as extremely severe, most offences being punishable with death. But in his laws on homicide, the part of the code which was preserved in force at Athens, Draco seems to have mitigated the law by allowing circumstances to be taken into consideration which reduced murder to justifiable homicide, and protecting from the violence of the avenger any one who, being banished for homicide, observed strictly the regulations imposed upon him. He also altered the court which pronounced sentence, by supplementing the old Basileis—*i.e.* the archon Basileus and the four Phylobasileis—with a body of fifty-one *Ephetae* or "Referees,"

---

[1] The inscription is on a papyrus, at Berlin. It is given in Gilbert's *Handbuch der Griechischen Staatsalterthümer*, pp. 123, 124.

with whom the final decision lay. These Ephetae sat at different places according to the nature of the offence. If the offence was wilful and premeditated, the court sat at the Areopagus; if accidental, at the Palladium, the temple of Athena on the Ilissus; if justifiable, at the Delphinium, or temple of Apollo, who had pleaded justification even in the case of Orestes. For the number of these Ephetae no satisfactory reason has been given.

The Attempt of Cylon.

The publication of the laws was probably made in order to satisfy the discontent of the lower orders of the people. The same cause may have led Cylon to embark on his attempt to establish a "tyranny" at Athens. He had moreover the example of his father-in-law, Theagenes of Megara, to stimulate him. In one of the Olympic years 620, 616, 612 (we can hardly decide which, but 620 is most probable), he seized the Acropolis, and attempted to hold it with the assistance of his friends. He expected, no doubt, that the mass of the people would join him, but, on the contrary, they flocked from the country to besiege him. Hunger compelled him to capitulate, and, though he escaped, numbers of his adherents were put to death—some in a sacrilegious manner at the altars of the gods and after a promise of safety had been given. Hence the Alcmaeonidae, who were held to be responsible for the slaughter, were known as the "accursed."

It is remarkable as a proof of the uncertainty of the early history of Athens, that Herodotus and Thucydides give discrepant accounts of this affair. Herodotus speaks of the prytanies of the naucraries as the important executive power in Athens at the time; Thucydides distinctly asserts that the nine archons "managed most of the public business"—(Hdt. v. 71, Thuc. i. 126).

The guilt of the murder of these conspirators, combined with the discontent of the people, rendered the condition of Athens more miserable than ever. To allay the first, Epimenides, a seer of Crete, who was considered to be of more than human origin, was summoned to Athens. By expiations and purifications, which were within the reach of all, he soothed the terrified spirits of the inhabitants. But the social misery required stronger remedies. It arose principally from the severe load of debt, and the high rate of interest. Men who had once borrowed became unable to extricate themselves; their obligations increased until not only their property passed into the hands of their creditors, but also their liberty, and that of their children. Thus native Athenians became slaves on the estates of their masters, and were even sold out of the country. In order to get rid of a state of affairs which was felt to be intolerable, Solon, the son of Exestides, a man of noble birth, but occupied in mercantile pursuits, was called upon to mediate between the two parties, 595 B.C.

The Seisachtheia of Solon

Solon adopted the extreme measure of a cancelling of debts. All money paid in interest was to be deducted from the principal sum which had been borrowed, and all debts secured upon the land or person of the debtor were cancelled. This at once restored the debtors to freedom and removed from the lands the stones which recorded the sums borrowed upon them. In order, it is said, to prevent this measure from pressing too heavily upon those who had money due to them, Solon also introduced a change of the coinage reducing the weight of the drachma by about 38 per cent., so that 73 of the old drachmas weighed as much as 100 of the new. Those therefore who had money to pay their debts—*i.e.* the somewhat richer classes, who were not reduced to borrowing on property or personal security—were able to pay them in the new coin instead of the old, and thus escaped the payment of about a third of the sum. At the same time those who received the money had a sum as large in coin as if they had received payment under the old standard. Those also who were not in debt, and perhaps were creditors of others, found their means increased by this alteration at the time when they were called upon to sacrifice what was due to them from indigent debtors. For the future it was illegal that any man should accept the person of the debtor as security for money lent. These measures, though at first received with discontent, were found effective in removing the evils, and in consequence increased the influence of Solon. He was now elected archon, and charged with the far more important duty of reforming and reconstructing the constitution of Athens. (594.)

The Constitution of Solon.

(A.) *Divisions of the people.*

The people were divided into four classes, according to their wealth:—

(1) *Pentecosiomedimni,* possessing not less than 500 measures of wheat (or wine and oil).
(2) *Hippeis,* . . do. 300 measures do.
(3) *Zeugitae,* . . do. 200 measures do.
(4) *Thetes,* possessing less than 200 measures do.

As this classification rests on the produce of *landed* property only, those who did not possess *land*, however wealthy in other respects, fell into the fourth class.

From the first class only were chosen the highest officers of state. From the first and second classes were chosen the cavalry. From the first three classes were chosen the hoplites or heavy-armed soldiers.

The members of the fourth class had a right to vote at the General Assembly, and to take part in trials by jury. They might also be called upon to serve as light-armed soldiers in the battle-field, or to man the fleet.

(B.) *Political Assemblies.*

(1) *The Ecclesia,* or General Assembly of the whole body of

Athenian citizens over twenty years of age. Nothing could be brought before this Assembly which had not been previously discussed by the Senate of Four Hundred. How often, or when the Assembly was summoned, we do not know.

(2) *The Council of Four Hundred,* composed of a hundred from each of the four tribes. This council may have taken the place of the board of the Prytanies of the Naucraries. It prepared matters for the General Assembly, and no doubt decided many things upon its own authority.

(C.) *Law and Justice.*

The nine archons were the chief administrators of the law, but there was also a *Heliaea,* or law-court before which cases were brought, when the authority of the archons was insufficient, or, perhaps, when it was contested.

Matters of homicide were decided by the *Council of the Areopagus,* with the assistance of the *Ephetae,* but the council was enlarged and remodelled. The nine archons, after their year of office, passed into it, and there remained for life. As the age qualifying for the archonship was thirty years, many men were members of the council for a great number of years, and as nine were added each year, the total would be large. This council was now supreme controller of the manners and discipline of the state, and the behaviour of the public officers. Under the Solonian constitution, no one received pay for attendance at the Assembly, or the Council, or the Heliaea.

Tyranny of Peisistratus.

The constitution of Solon was, after a time, followed by renewed *factions,* owing to which Peisistratus was enabled to make himself tyrant of Athens. After being twice expelled, he succeeded in firmly establishing his power, which he bequeathed to his son Hippias. The government of Peisistratus is said to have been mild and equitable, in the first instance (Hdt. i. 59 : οὔτε τιμὰς τὰς ἐούσας συνταράξας οὔτε θέσμια μεταλλάξας, ἐπί τε τοῖσι κατεστεῶσι ἔνεμε τὴν πολιν κοσμέων καλῶς τε καὶ εὖ). Afterwards he found it necessary to support his power by a large bodyguard (Hdt. i. 64). His tyranny was highly distasteful to men of power and eminence, so that Miltiades preferred to leave the city and dwell in the Chersonese (Hdt. vi. 35). The rule of the sons of Peisistratus was more severe, specially after the death of Hipparchus in 514 (Hdt. v. 55). The whole result was disastrous to the energy and union of the people. Hippias was expelled in 510 B.C., with the help of the Lacedaemonians, and after some party quarrels between Cleisthenes, the leader of the Alcmaeonid family, and Isagoras, Cleisthenes expelled his opponents, and established a more democratic form of constitution.

Constitution of Cleisthenes.

(1) Removing the old division into four tribes, he divided the people into *ten tribes*, and a hundred demes, allotting ten demes to a tribe. In some cases the demes in the same tribe were not contiguous, to prevent local union.

(2) He raised the *Council* from 400 to 500, *i.e.* fifty from each tribe, and probably increased the number of the officers on various boards to ten,[1] *i.e.* one for each tribe.

(3) He introduced the plan of *ostracism*, by which the people were enabled to get rid of a dangerous citizen, if 6000 votes were given against him in the Assembly.

It is possible that Cleisthenes introduced the system of electing officers by *lot*; at any rate, this system would seem to have been in use at the time of the battle of Marathon.

This form of constitution gave great encouragement to the people, who showed themselves worthy of their freedom in the Persian war.

---

[1] For instance, we find ten generals at the battle of Marathon, which denotes a change from the old system under which the army was controlled by the archon polemarch.

Changes after the Persian War.

(1) On the motion of Aristides, the highest offices were thrown open to all the Solonian classes.

(2) Pay was introduced, first in the Heliaea, and secondly in the Assembly, the sum being gradually increased. The members of the Council were also paid (*see* Thuc. viii. 69).

(3) The authority of the Areopagus was much curtailed.

By these means the Athenian constitution became an extreme form of Democracy, in which the people were sovereign. The important check upon their action which still remained in force was the rule that every measure brought before the Assembly must have been previously discussed in the Council. The importance of the Law Courts greatly increased, the jury being paid, and the allies in the Delian Confederacy compelled to bring their suits to Athens.

Changes after the Sicilian Expedition.

This great disaster caused a party among the Athenians to attempt some reforms, in the hope of restricting the extreme form of Democracy—

(1) A body of Probouli was established—413 B.C. (Thuc. viii. 1).

(2) On the proposal of Peisander and Antiphon, 400 men are chosen to manage the state, the Council of Five Hundred is removed, the Assembly restricted to 5000 men. No one is to receive pay except the soldiers (Thuc. viii. 67)—411 B.C.

This form of constitution continued but a few months.

(3.) The 400 are removed, and 5000 citizens, able to provide themselves with armour, are chosen to form the Assembly and manage the state. New laws are passed, the government being wisely and equitably administered (Thuc. viii. 97.)

(4) The moderate form of government is set aside; five ephors are chosen to preside at the Assemblies; and, finally, after the capture of Athens by Sparta, the *Thirty Tyrants* are

established. Though intended to remodel the constitution, they merely governed at their own caprice, putting to death all who appeared in any way likely to oppose their action.

(5) Owing to the heroism of Thrasybulus and a band of exiles the Thirty Tyrants were expelled, and the ancient constitution restored (403 B.C.). The laws were revised; the authority of the Areopagus restored; and an amnesty provided for all Athenians except the Thirty Tyrants and the Committee of Ten, who, being chosen to administer the state immediately after their expulsion, had proved little better than the Thirty Tyrants themselves.

From this time the Athenian constitution remained in form the same. The people became more and more disinclined to undertake public burdens; above all, they allowed their battles to be fought for them by mercenary troops. For this reason, added to the ineradicable evil of disunion, which prevented the Greeks from forming any satisfactory form of national league, they fell an easy prey to the power of Macedon.

Final Form of the Constitution.

(A.) *The Council of Five Hundred.*

These were chosen by lot, from all classes of the citizens who possessed full rights and were over thirty years of age. They received as payment a drachma per diem, and were re-eligible. For each place two candidates were taken by lot; every candidate who failed to pass the examination ($\delta o \kappa \iota \mu a \sigma i a$) was rejected, and the second in the list took his place. They held office for a year, at the conclusion of which it was customary for the Assembly to decree a crown to the Council.

Their duties consisted in :—

(*a.*) Preparing measures for discussion in the Assembly, where nothing could be discussed except on their initiation.

(*b.*) Managing the revenues of the state.

(*c.*) Superintending the building of ships, and other matters in connection with the navy.

(*d.*) Superintending the cavalry.

(*e.*) Examining the candidates for the office of archon.

(*f.*) They had also a certain amount of judicial power, which enabled them to receive complaints and inflict fines up to the amount of fifty drachmae.

The Council met daily, but, to avoid the inconvenience of keeping together 500 men, it was divided by tribes; the fifty men (πρυτάνεις) from each of the ten tribes remaining in office for a tenth part of a year (πρυτάνεια). These prytanies lived at the public expense in the prytaneum (Tholus), during their term of office.

The fifty prytanies of each tribe and the term of their office were again subdivided, ten prytanies being in office for seven days, who were known as πρόεδροι, and each day one of the proedri was chosen as epistates. But with these proedri sat nine others, one from each of the nine tribes, who were also known as proedri.

Note (1).—The Attic year ordinarily consisted of 354 days, which gives 35 days for six prytanies and 36 for four. But in the years when there was an intercalary month the length of the prytanies became 38 and 39 days.

Note (2).—At a later time (see 345 B.C.) one of the tribes was allotted to support the prytanies in the Assemblies. This is the προεδρεύουσα φυλή.

(*B.*) *The Assembly.*

The Assembly consisted of all genuine Athenians of more than twenty years of age.

Meetings were of two kinds.

(*a.*) The regular meetings (κυρίαι), of which there were four in each prytany.

(*b.*) The extraordinary meetings (σύγκλητοι), convened for the despatch of some special business.

The place of meeting was originally the market-place; then the Pnyx; at times the people met in the Theatre, or even outside Athens. The prytanies, or, on extraordinary occasions, the generals, summoned the meetings. Every Athenian attending received a ticket which enabled him to receive from the Thesmothetae the obol (and finally three obols) for attendance.

The business of the meeting was introduced by one of the prytanies or proedri, and sometimes by one of the generals. The citizens were called on to speak in order of age. Votes were given either by show of hands ($\chi\epsilon\iota\rho\text{o}\tau\text{o}\nu\epsilon\hat{\iota}\nu$, $\chi\epsilon\iota\rho\text{o}\tau\text{o}\nu\iota\alpha$) or by ballot, the former being the usual method. When a decree was proposed, and even when it had been passed, its further progress could be stopped if any citizen affirmed on oath that he would indict the proposer for bringing forward an illegal measure. (In this manner Aeschines checked the proposal of Ctesiphon to crown Demosthenes in 337 B.C.) In cases which involved ostracism, banishment, and the like, the ballot was always used, and not less than 6000 votes were required to make the decision effective. The meeting was put off if any unfavourable sign were noticed, rain, thunder, and the like ($\delta\iota\text{o}\sigma\eta\mu\iota\alpha$).

Legislative Powers of the Assembly.

An ordinary decree of the Assembly was a $\psi\dot\eta\phi\iota\sigma\mu\alpha$, which is quite different from a $\nu\acute\text{o}\mu\text{o}\varsigma$. Legislation, *i.e.* the management of the laws, was thus arranged:—

In the first meeting of each year the question was put whether the old laws were to be retained or any change made, the Thesmothetae having meanwhile revised the laws, and exhibited on tablets in a public place any which seemed to be contradictory or unsatisfactory. Beside these were hung the laws which it was proposed to add to the statute-book. In the third meeting 1000 Nomothetae were selected from the jurors of the year (*i.e.* men over thirty years of age, who had taken the Heliastic oath). Before these the case of the laws was argued, speakers being chosen to support the old laws, and the proposers advocating the new. The laws which won the most votes were retained or adopted. In later times this strict procedure was in part abandoned, and laws were passed much in the same manner as decrees.

Elective Functions.

With the Assembly also rested the election of those magistrates who were not chosen by lot. This took place on the ἀρχαιρεσίαι, or election days. Moreover, on the first meeting in every prytany, the people were asked whether they wished the existing officers to be continued in office or not (ἐπιχειροτονία τῶν ἀρχόντων).

Judicial Functions.

Before the Assembly were tried the cases which either involved danger to those who brought them forward or were of special importance. Thus μηνύσεις, or "informations," were laid before the people. A special form of accusation was the εἰσαγγελία, which also took place before the Assembly, and the προβολή, by which an injured person attempted to secure popular favour on his side (as Demosthenes in his suit against Midias). Ostracism could only take place in the Assembly.

The Assembly was the supreme authority of the state. Its decision was final on all matters of war and peace, on the nomination of generals, the destination of armies and fleets, the application of the public funds, the honours to be decreed to citizens or foreigners. Though it had no power of initiative, it alone had the power of ratification and final decision.

(C.) The Executive.

The executive officers at Athens were very numerous. Those who occupied places requiring special knowledge were chosen by show of hands, not by lot. Before entering office, they had to pass an examination as to birth and character (δοκιμασία), and those who failed lost their rights as citizens. At the end of office each had to give in an account of any money which he had received from the public, or to state that he had not received any (εὔθυναι).

The action of the officers was limited: (1) by the short tenure of office, and the accounts to be given in at the end; (2) by the suspension which might be pronounced in any prytany during the year of office ; (3) by the division of authority among boards, usually of ten ; (4) by the constant intervention of the Assembly by decrees, etc. Nor were the officers treated with much respect, or their wishes and views consulted.

The principal officers at Athens were :—

(*a.*) *Judicial.*

    The Nine Archons, of whom :—

        The Archon was engaged chiefly with matters of family law, inheritance, adoption, etc.

        The Basileus with matters of homicide, etc.

        The Polemarch with matters affecting foreigners.

        The Six Thesmothetae with cases not falling to the other three.

    The Eleven, who formed as it were the criminal police.

    The Astynomi, who took charge of the city, public morals, etc.

    The Agoranomi, who superintended the markets.

    The Metronomi, or superintendents of weights and measures.

    The Sitophylaces, who regulated the prices of corn, etc.

(*b.*) *Financial.*

    The Poletae, who superintended the leasing of public property.

    The Practores, who got in fines, etc.

    The Apodectae, or receivers-general of public funds.

    The Colacretae, who supplied funds to the Prytaneum.

    The treasurers of the Goddess (Athena) who kept accounts of the public treasury.

    The Minister of Finance, ὁ ἐπὶ τῇ διοικήσει.

(*c.*) *Military.*

    (*a.*) Strategí and Taxiarchi.

    (*b.*) Hipparchi and Phylarchi (officers of cavalry).

    The generals were also supreme over the fleet, which was, however, supplied by the system of *trierarchies*.

(D.) The Administration of Law.

The enactment of laws, as we have seen, was the business of the Assembly; their administration was carried out by the Heliaea or jury, the Diaetetae or arbitrators, the Areopagus, and the Ephetae. To an insignificant extent the Council of 500 and the Archons possessed judicial powers.

(a.) The Heliaea. This is one of the most remarkable institutions of Athens. Each year the nine Archons selected by lot, from the number of those who presented themselves for the office, six thousand men, *i.e.* six hundred from each tribe as jurors. The qualification for the office was that a man should be an Athenian citizen, and more than thirty years of age. Of the 6,000, 5,000 were distributed into ten companies of 500 each, the remaining thousand being retained as a supplementary body, to fill up deficiencies. On his election every juror took the "Heliastic" oath, and received a tablet marked with his own name, with the symbols of the owl and Gorgon's head, and with the letter of the company to which he belonged. When their services were needed, they were assembled by the Thesmothetae in the market-place, and lots were cast to determine in what law-court (δικαστήριον), and under what officer each man should serve. The numbers allotted to try a case differed, but care was taken that in no case should there be an even number. When the lots were over, each juryman received a staff marked with the colour and the letter of the court in which he was to serve. On entering the court he received a ticket, which, when he left, he presented to the Colacretae, from whom he received his pay. The courts were presided over by the Archons.

(b.) The Arbitrators were a number of citizens selected equally from each tribe by lot. They took the same oath as the jurors, but were not less than fifty years of age. They could decide suits, even on appeal from the jurors: at the end of the year they had to give in an account of their office. Even in the year any one who considered that they had acted

unjustly was at liberty to bring an impeachment (εἰσαγγελία) against them. Distinct from these were the Arbitrators, who went round the country inquiring into and deciding cases of assault and the like.

Before being brought before the Heliaea, or the Arbitrators, a complaint was investigated by one of the Archons, according to the nature of the case, who decided whether it was genuine, took the depositions, etc., and arranged for the trial before the jurors in the proper court.

(c.) From the time of Solon all cases of wilful murder, poisoning, wounding with intent, and arson, were tried before the court of the *Areopagus*. The trial was held in the open air, the King Archon presiding. Advocates were not allowed: the accuser and accused spoke on oath, two days being allowed for the statement of the case and the reply. On the third day, the votes were given by ballot. If the votes were equal, the accused was acquitted. The punishment of murder was death; of intent, banishment from the country; but the accused might retire from the trial after the first day and leave the country.

(d.) The process before the *Ephetae* was much the same as that before the Areopagus. But these judges, who were fifty-one in number, did not, at least after Solon's time, sit on the Areopagus, or judge cases of wilful murder. They sat at the Delphinium, or Palladium, or Phreattys, as the case might be, to judge offences of homicide which fell short of wilful murder. At the Phreattys, which was a place on the sea-shore, the Ephetae heard the cases of those who, being under sentence of banishment for homicide, wished to plead their defence. As these were forbidden the country, they were allowed to approach the shore in a boat, where the Ephetae met them.

CONSTITUTION OF LACEDAEMON.

Divisions of the People.

THE Dorians of Lacedaemon were an immigrant tribe who had established themselves in Peloponnesus by the conquest of the old Achaean inhabitants. The wars in which they accomplished this conquest were long and serious; in some cases the Dorians admitted their defeated enemies to a modified political independence, in others they reduced them to a state of complete serfdom. But the whole government was in Dorian hands, and the Lacedaemonian constitution applies only to them. The subjects were divided into—

(1) *Helots*, a name which is said to be derived from the town of Helus, the last city subdued by the Spartans. This was the lowest and most numerous class of subjects, especially after the conquest of Messenia. They were not so much slaves as serfs, the property of the state rather than individuals, for their masters could not sell them, and a public act was required for their manumission. They lived on plots of land, paying a certain fixed sum to the owners. They accompanied their masters to battle (at Plataea each Spartan was attended by seven Helots), rendered him service in other ways, and even served as light-armed soldiers in the army, and as sailors in the fleet. On rare occasions they were allowed to serve as heavy-armed soldiers. Though the Helots do not appear to have been in abject poverty, their lot was regarded as a very hard one. The Spartans were in constant terror of a rising, and took severe measures to prevent it. The Crypteia was a kind of detective service in which Spartan youths were sent round the

country to keep watch on the Helots and remove any one who appeared to be plotting against the state. On the other hand Helots who had shown bravery in the Spartan cause were sometimes allowed their liberty—though 2000 who claimed it on this score in the Peloponnesian war disappeared, "no one knew how" (Thuc. iv. 80)—and the children of Helots were at times brought up as Spartans (*Mothakes*). Helots who had received their liberty were called νεοδαμώδεις.

(2) *Perioeci*. These were the ancient Achaeans, who, probably because they made less resistance than the Messenians and others, were allowed more favourable terms. They lived in towns, and appear to have managed their own affairs; but they were governed by officers sent each year from Sparta, to which city they also paid tribute. They served in the army, constituting in fact the larger part of the heavy-armed soldiers. But they were in no sense members of the Spartan community. In the time of Polydorus the Perioeci were said to have numbered 30,000.

(3) *Spartans*. These, like all Dorians, were divided into three tribes, the Hylleis, Dymanes, and Pamphyli. Each of these tribes was divided into ten *obes*, which were again subdivided into οἶκοι or families. In the reign of Polydorus the number of these families is said to have been 9000. There was no distinction of classes as at Athens, at any rate in the best times of Sparta. All the citizens were regarded as equal (ὅμοιοι), and each house or family had a certain amount of land, sufficient at the least to provide the master of it with means enough to support his place as a citizen. But the difficulty of harmonising property and population was deeply felt, and in time the citizens became fewer and fewer, while the land was owned by a comparatively small number of proprietors. These difficulties, which arose partly from the unequal number of children in families, partly from the deaths in war or other calamities, were increased by the law of Epitadeus, by which it became possible to sell or give away

the plots of land which had hitherto been inalienable. Hence, in the time of Agis III., the citizens were divided into Homoei (ὅμοιοι) and Hypomeiones (Inferiors); the number of Spartans was 700 only, and the land was in the possession of 100 owners.

Lycurgus.

The Spartans regarded their constitution as the work of *Lycurgus*. But of Lycurgus little was known even in antiquity that was certain. The dates of his life differ (see Tables); and authorities are not agreed what part of the constitution of Sparta is really his work. He is universally regarded as putting an end to a period of strife and sedition. Hence it is probable that he curtailed the power of the kings—Aristotle (*Politics*, 5. 12), speaks of the tyranny of Charilaus changing into an aristocracy—and gave greater authority to the nobles and people. This is perhaps all that we can ascribe to him; the training (at any rate in the details), the Ephors, and arrangement of the army were later.

The Kings.

Sparta was unique in possessing a double monarchy. The two kings, according to the legend, were descended from the twin sons of Aristodemus, one of the three Heracleids who conducted the invasion into the Peloponnesus. The elder line was known as the Eurystheids, or Agiads, the younger as the Proclids or Eurypontids. Of this extraordinary arrangement no satisfactory explanation can be given; it may be conjectured—

(1) That the two kings represent a Dorian and an Achaean community which came to terms with each other, retaining their separate monarchs.

(2) That they represent two Dorian communities, who after a period of strife united at Sparta.

(3) That they represent two eminent families whose claims to precedence, after causing much strife, were at length compromised by admitting both to the monarchy.

The two lines of kings had separate burial-places, and did not intermarry. Herodotus tells us that the two sons of Aristodemus quarrelled all their lives and their descendants had done the same.

Duties of the Kings.

(1) *As Priests.* They were the Priests of Zeus Lacedaemonius and Zeus Uranius. They were summoned to all public sacrifices and received a double portion of food. They also received the skins of the victims. In war they offered sacrifice on the part of the people (Hdt. vi. 56).

(2) *Judges.* They decided in the cases of heiresses (πατρούχου παρθένου πέρι) who were claimed by one or more relatives, and adoptions were made in their presence. They were also charged with the superintendence of the public roads.

(3) *Military Commanders.* In war they were the commanders-in-chief. Originally both kings went out with the army, but afterwards only one was sent. Their powers were gradually curtailed. Two of the Ephors accompanied them to the field, and, at times, their power was limited by commissioners who accompanied them on their expeditions. Moreover, they were liable to be brought to trial by the Ephors for their conduct. In more than one instance we find kings deposed by the Ephors.

The Gerontes.

These were twenty-eight in number, forming, together with the kings, a council of thirty. As this number corresponds to that of the obes, it is probable that each obe had a representative in the Assembly, an arrangement which also implies that the two kings belonged to two separate obes. The Gerontes were men over sixty years of age, and held their office for life. They were elected by acclamation. We have little information about their duties. Cases involving the life of a citizen were brought before them;

and they had some jurisdiction over the kings. To what extent their sentences required to be confirmed by the popular Assembly is doubtful.

The Assembly or Halia.

According to the *Rhetra* of Lycurgus given in Plutarch's life, the Assembly was to be convened at stated times between two fixed points, Babyke and Knakion, at Sparta. The people thus assembled were to have the right of accepting or refusing the measures brought before them, but discussion was not allowed. At a later time, in the reign of King Theopompus, the Kings and Gerontes seem to have succeeded in taking from the people their right of control (αἰ δὲ σκολιὰν ὁ δᾶμος ἕλοιτο, τοὺς πρεσβυγενέας καὶ ἀρχαγέτας ἀποστατῆρας εἶμεν). If this was so, it is certain that the people afterwards recovered it. The Assembly was composed of Spartans over thirty years of age. The votes were given by acclamation, but in Thuc. i. 87 we find an instance in which the Assembly was asked to divide upon a question. The matters brought before the Assembly were questions of peace and war, the enactment of laws, manumission of Helots, election of magistrates, etc.

The Ephors.

The time at which the Ephors were instituted at Sparta is uncertain, some ascribing the office to Lycurgus, others (Aristotle among the number) to Theopompus, others again to Chilon. In the first instance the Ephors seem to have been charged with the settlement of petty disputes, but by degrees they became the most powerful body in the state, so that some thought them a tyrannical element in the Lacedaemonian constitution. They were five in number, elected from the people, even the very poorest being chosen. They held office for a year, and were irresponsible. Though they do not seem to have had the power to pass sentence of death, they controlled almost every department of the constitution. We find them sending out armies, accompanying the kings on their expeditions, bringing kings to justice for misconduct, and interfering with their marriages, etc. They also, in the last resort, superintended the training of the children and young citizens. Though in many respects the ephoralty is condemned by Aristotle, he allows that it was owing to it that the constitution remained so long unaltered (*Pol.* 5. 11). The first Ephor, like the first archon at Athens, gave his name to the year.

The Training.

But the distinctive feature of the Spartan constitution was the training of the Spartan youth, both male and female. To whom this elaborate system, in which a Spartan was regarded as existing for the state only, and trained for that service, is due cannot be fixed with certainty. In its full extent it probably belongs to the period after the Messenian wars, and may have been largely developed from some ancient germs by Chilon.

From the moment of birth a Spartan child was the object of public solicitude. It was left to a select body of elders to decide whether the infant was worth rearing or not. If not, it was exposed; if it was strong and healthy, it was reared by the mother till the age of seven, when the public training began. The children were under the superintendence of Paedonomi, but the youngest were associated with those older than themselves, these again with others still older, in order that they might learn by example, no less than instruction. They practised various gymnastic exercises; when sufficiently strong they went out hunting; and were stimulated by competitive trials of skill, strength, and agility. In order to test their endurance, boys were whipped at the altar of Athena Orthosia, a process under which some are said to have died. The amount of food allowed was purposely insufficient in order that the boys might add to it by hunting or even theft, which was only punished when detected. After the age of twelve but one garment was allowed, and neither head nor feet were covered. From the age of twenty to thirty the Spartans were called εἴρενες.

Of intellectual training they received very little. They were trained in Dorian musical measures, and learned certain poems which were thought suitable, especially the songs of Terpander. Besides this they were allowed to be present at the conversations and discussions of the older men, in order to hear specimens of Laconian wit and brevity. Every influence which could in any way excite them to distinguish themselves in the exercises assigned to them was brought to bear upon them. The training of the girls was naturally less severe than that of the boys, but they also practised gymnastic exercises, and were incited to excellence by competitions in public.

The training came to an end at the age of thirty. But the Spartan even then was not his own master. He was indeed allowed to have his own house and wife (if he married earlier, he could only visit his wife in secret) but he could not take his meals at home. He had to be present at the Syssitia or common meals provided under public supervision (φιδίτια is the Laconian name), where only a prescribed kind and amount of food was allowed. To this meal each citizen contributed a quota, on the payment of which rested his position as a citizen. Any one who failed to pay was no longer a member of the Spartan body. For those who in the degenerate days of Greece regarded individual licence as the source of all evil, and a strict education as the best remedy for impending ruin, Sparta offered peculiar attractions. Here the lawgiver had succeeded in moulding according to his will the minds and bodies of a community. Their lives and the most important relations of life were controlled by the state, and dedicated to the service of the community. The bravery of the Spartans was an accepted fact in Hellas; they were never known to fly; and in their steadfast courage the effect of their training was most apparent. Every precaution was taken to prevent the high standard from being contaminated by luxury. There was no coinage in Sparta; the utmost simplicity of dress was demanded from rich and poor alike. Strangers were received with caution and mistrust. But the system nevertheless broke down; the equality of the citizens became a fiction rather than a reality, fewer and fewer were found able or willing to undergo the training. The selfish use which Sparta made of her supremacy after the fall of Athens roused a strong feeling against her, and with the loss of Messenia a great portion of the land (from which came the funds necessary for the maintenance of the Syssitia) was lost also. From this time dates the rapid decline of Sparta, whose system of government appears to have had far less attraction for Aristotle than it had exercised in a previous generation on Plato and Xenophon.

INDEX

TO THE CHRONOLOGICAL TABLES.

(The Numbers denote the years B.C.)

A

Abdera founded by Clazomenae, 654.
Abydus founded by Miletus, 715.
—— revolts from Athens, 411.
—— battle at, 411.
—— Pharnabazus repulsed at, 409.
Acanthus, in Chalcidice, founded by Andros, 654.
—— and Apollonia ask help from Sparta against Olynthus, 383.
Acarnania, Phormio makes an expedition into, 429.
—— invaded by Agesilaus, 390.
Acarnanians, the, occupy Anactorium, 425.
Achaea joins the Athenian alliance, 454.
Achaeans, the, of Calydon apply to Lacedaemon for help against the Acarnanians, 391.
Acragas (Agrigentum) founded by the Geloans, 582.
Actium, the Corcyreans conquer the Corinthians at, 435.
Aeaces restored to Samos by the Persians, 494.
Aegina taken by Dorians, 1074.
—— at war with Athens, 491.
—— besieged by the Athenians, 458.
—— reduced by the Athenians, 456.
—— at war with Athens, 389.
Aeginetans, the, join the Thebans against Athens, and attack Attica, 507.

Aeginetans expelled from Aegina, 431.
Aegospotami, Lysander defeats the Athenians at, 405.
Aeolian colonies in Asia Minor founded, 1054.
Aeschines, the orator, at Mantinea, 362.
—— "Against Timarchus," 345.
—— "On the False Legation," 343.
—— "On the Crown," 330.
—— at the Amphictyonic Assembly with Midias, 339.
Aeschylus at the battle of Marathon, 490.
—— "Persae," 472.
—— "Oresteia," 458.
—— dies, 456.
Aesopus (fable-poet), 570.
Agathon, the tragic poet, wins the prize at the Lenaea, 416.
Agesilaus becomes king in Sparta 399.
—— sets out for Asia, 396.
—— collects his army at Ephesus, 395.
—— marches on Sardis, 395.
—— makes an alliance with Cotys, 395.
—— is recalled, 394.
—— invades Corinth, 392.
—— invades Argolis, 391.
—— ravages the country of the Acarnanians, 391.
—— prepares to invade Acarnania again, 390.

Agesilaus besieges Phlius, 380.
—— refuses to go on the expedition to Thebes, 379.
—— dies, 357.
Agesipolis dies at Aphytis, 380.
Agis invades Attica the fifth time, 425.
—— makes incursions from Deceleia, 413.
—— invades Elis, 401.
—— invades Elis the second time, 400.
—— dies at Lacedaemon, 399.
Agis II. heads a revolt in Peloponnesus, but is crushed and slain by Antipater, 330.
Agnon colonises Amphipolis, 437.
Agrigentum, siege and capture of, 406.
Alalia founded by Phocaea, 564.
Alcaeus of Mitylene, 610.
Alcamenes, king of Sparta, 743.
"*Alcestis*," the, of Euripides, 438.
Alcibiades attacked for offences against the mysteries, 415.
—— sails to Sicily, but is recalled and goes to Argos, 415.
—— intrigues with the Samian oligarchs for his return, 411.
—— returns to Samos, 411.
—— recalled, 411.
—— escapes from Sardis, 410.
—— gains Selymbria and Chalcedon for Athens, 409.
—— is chosen general though exiled, 408.
—— is deposed from the generalship, 407.
—— death of, 404.
Alcidas takes 42 ships to Mitylene, 427.
Alcmaeonids expelled from Athens, 599.
Alcman, the lyric poet, lived at Sparta about 671.
Alexander of Pherae takes Samos, and defeats the Athenians at Peparethus, 362.
—— assassinated, 359.
Alexander the Great born 356.

Alexander the Great and Olympias leave Macedonia, 337.
—— succeeds in Macedon, 336.
—— besieges and captures Thebes, 335.
—— takes Miletus, 334.
—— passes into Persia, 334.
—— falls ill at Tarsus, 333.
—— pursues Darius to Ecbatana, 330.
—— subjugates Sogdiana, 329-327.
—— demands divine honours, 327.
—— proceeds to Bactria and marries Roxana, 327.
—— captures Bessus, whom he puts to death, and massacres the Branchidae, 329.
—— marches to Babylon, is taken ill and dies, 323.
Alexandria, foundation of, 332.
Alyattes succeeds Sadyattes in Lydia, 617.
Amasis dethrones Apries, king of Egypt, 570.
Ambracia founded by Corinth, 625.
Amphictyonic war, 339.
Amphilochian Argos attacked by Spartans and Ambraciots, 426.
Amphipolis, Athenians attempt to colonise, 465.
—— colonised by Agnon, 437.
—— taken by Brasidas, 424.
—— is retained by Lacedaemon, 421.
—— attacked by Athens and Perdiccas, 414.
—— besieged by Philip, 358.
Amyntas I., king of Macedonia, 540.
—— offers Anthemus to Hippias, 510.
Amyntas II., king of Macedonia, 389.
Anacharsis, the Scythian, said to have visited Athens about 592.
Anacreon of Teos, 543.
Anactorium founded by Corinth, 625.
—— occupied by the Acarnanians, 425.

Anaxagoras leaves Athens, 450.
—— the philosopher, 448.
Anaxandridas and Ariston, kings of Sparta, 560.
Anaxibius supersedes Dercyllidas at Abydus, 389.
—— defeated and slain by Iphicrates, 389.
Anaxilaus of Rhegium, 493.
Anaximander of Miletus, 592.
Anaximenes of Miletus, 546.
Andocides, the orator, 391.
Antalcidas is sent to Tiribazus, the general of the king, to propose peace, 392.
—— goes to Ephesus and joins Tiribazus, 389.
—— prevents the corn ships from sailing to Athens, 388.
—— the peace of, 387.
Antandrus taken by Athens, 424.
Antimachus of Teus, 753.
Antiphanes, the comic poet, 343.
Antiphon executed, 411.
Antisthenes, the philosopher, 399.
Apollonia founded by Corinth, 625.
Apries, king of Egypt, dethroned by Amasis, 570.
Aracus is sent out as admiral, 405.
Arbela, Alexander defeats Darius at, 331.
Arcadians, the, celebrate the Olympic festival with the Pisatans, 364.
—— use the sacred money, but the Mantineans refuse to do so, 363.
Arcesilaus I. succeeds Battus I. in Cyrene, 591.
Archias of Corinth founds Syracuse, 734.
Archidamus II., king of Sparta, 469.
Archidamus III. succeeds Agesilaus in Sparta, 357 (361).
Archilochus of Paros, 700.
Arctinus of Miletus, 776.
Ardys, king of Lydia, 678-629.
Areopagus, the, weakened by Pericles and Ephialtes, 460.
Arginusae, Peloponnesians defeated at the, 406.

Argive democracy put down, 418.
—— oligarchy defeated by the popular party, 417.
Argolis, invasion of, by Cleomenes, 520.
—— invasion of, by Epidaurus, 418.
Argos and Sparta at war, 669.
—— and Epidaurus at war, 419.
—— and Lacedaemon, peace between, 418.
—— the Scytalism at, 370.
Ariobarzanes tries to bring about peace between the Thebans and Lacedaemonians, 368.
Arion of Methymna in Lesbos, 625.
Aristagoras attacks Naxos, 501.
—— revolts from Persia, 500.
—— retires to Myrcinus and is slain, 497.
Aristeides, archon at Athens, 489.
—— ostracised, 483.
—— proposes that the 4th Solonian class should be allowed to hold office, 477.
—— death of, 468.
Aristippus, the philosopher, 399.
Ariston and Anaxandridas, kings of Sparta, 560.
Aristophanes, the "Banqueters" of, 427.
—— the "Babylonians" of, 426.
—— the "Acharnians" of, 425.
—— the "Knights" of, 424.
—— the "Clouds" of, 423.
—— the "Wasps" of, 422.
—— the "Peace" of, 421.
—— the "Birds" of, 414.
—— the "Lysistrata" and "Thermophoriazusae" of, 411.
—— the "Frogs" of, 405.
—— the "Ecclesiazusae" of, 392.
—— the "Plutus" of, 388.
Aristotle, birth of, 384.
—— summoned to the Macedonian court, 342.
—— death of, 322.
Arnaeans driven into Boeotia, 1123.
Artaphernes, a Persian, captured at Eion, 425.

Artaxerxes I. succeeds Xerxes, 465.
—— death of, 425.
Artaxerxes II. succeeds Darius II., 405.
Artemisia succeeds Mausolus in Caria, 351.
Artemisium, seafight at, 480.
Asine conquered by the Argives, 761.
Astyages defeated by Cyrus, 559.
Atarneus besieged by Dercyllidas, 397.
Athenian Cleruchi, first instance of at Chalcis, 507.
—— empire, rise of, 476.
—— army and fleet defeated in Egypt, 455.
—— embassy to Samos, 411.
—— the, oligarchs make proposals of peace to Sparta, 411.
Athenians at war with Corinth, Epidaurus, and Aegina, 458.
—— the, form an alliance with Sitalces, 431.
—— the, capture Cythera, 424.
—— the, retake Scione, 421.
—— the, under Pythodorus attack Laconia, 414.
—— the, take tolls from ships passing through the Hellespont, 410.
—— the, help to rebuild the walls of Corinth, 391.
—— the, put to death one of the generals who assisted the Thebans and banish the other, 379.
—— the, build gates to the Peiraeus, 378.
—— the, make peace with Sparta, 369.
—— the, and the Phliasians make peace with Thebes, 366.
—— the, declare war on Philip, 340.
Athens, decennial archons at, 752.
—— nine yearly archons at, 683.
—— at war with Aegina, 491.
—— occupied by the Persians, 480.
—— rebuilt and surrounded by a wall, 478.

Athens abandons the empire by land, 445.
—— and Sparta at peace for 30 years, 445.
—— founds Thurii, 443.
—— forms a defensive alliance with Corcyra, 433.
—— plague breaks out at, 430.
—— takes Antandrus, 424.
—— forms an alliance with the Argive confederacy (exc. the Corinthians), 420.
—— Lacedaemon declares war on, 413.
—— proposes peace to Agis, which he refuses, 411.
—— revolution at, 411.
—— blockaded by land and sea, 405.
—— sends ambassadors to Agis to treat for peace, 405.
—— the Thirty established at, 404.
——walls of, rebuilt by Conon, 393.
—— at war with Aegina, 389.
—— reform in finance at, 378.
—— the allies revolt from, Social War, 358-356.
—— at war with Philip, 357.
—— makes peace with Olynthus, 352.
Attica first invaded by Archidamus, 431.
—— invaded by the Peloponnesians for the second time, 430.
—— invaded for the third time, 428.
—— invaded for the fourth time, 427.
—— invaded for the fifth time, 425.
Autocles is sent from Athens to the Hellespont to secure the corn supplies, 361.
Automenes, king of Corinth, deposed, 745.

B

Babylon became independent of Assyria under Nabopolassar, 625.

Babylon taken by Cyrus, 538.
Bacchylides, the lyric poet, 480.
Battus I. founds Cyrene, 631.
Battus II. of Cyrene succeeds Arcesilaus I., 575.
Bessus conspires against Alexander, 330.
Boeotia evacuated by the Athenians, 447.
—— plot formed for the invasion of, 424.
—— invaded for the first time by the Spartans under Cleombrotus, 378.
—— invaded the second time by the Spartans under Agesilaus, 378.
—— invaded the third time by the Lacedaemonians under Agesilaus, 377.
—— invaded the fourth time by the Peloponnesians under Cleombrotus, 376.
Boeotians, the, take possession of Heraclea, 419.
—— the, ally themselves with Lacedaemon, 421.
Borysthenes founded by Miletus, 654.
Brasidas takes Torone, 424.
—— takes Amphipolis, 424.
—— fails in an attempt on Potidaea, 423.
—— captures Scione, 423.
—— death of, 422.
Byzantians supported by Athens, 390.
Byzantium founded by the Megarians, 657.
—— conquest of, 476.
—— revolt, 411.
—— is betrayed to the Athenians, 409.
—— and Athens, alliance between, 341.

C

Calliades archon at Athens, 480.
Callias in Susa, 444.

Callicratidas succeeds Lysander, 407.
—— killed at Arginusae, 406.
Callinus the elegiac poet, 715.
Callisthenes is killed for opposing Alexander's demand for divine honours, 327.
Callistratus banished from Athens, 361.
Camarina founded by Syracuse, 599.
—— destroyed by Syracuse, 553.
Cambyses succeeds Cyrus, 529.
—— king of Persia, dies, 521.
Carnaean festival at Sparta is founded, 676.
Carthaginians defeated at Himera, 480.
—— in Sicily massacred, 397.
—— the, take Messene, 395.
Carystus conquered by the Athenians, 470.
Casmenae founded by Syracuse, 644.
Catana founded by Naxos, 730.
—— the Carthaginians successful in an engagement off, 395.
Cersobleptes succeeds Cotys in Thrace, 360.
Chabrias defeats Gorgopas in Aegina, 389.
—— defeats the Peloponnesian fleet at Naxos, 376.
—— returns from Egypt to Athens, 359.
—— is killed at the battle of Chios, 358.
Chaeronea, battle of, 338.
Chalcedon founded by Megara, 675.
Chalcis and Athens, alliance between, 342.
Chares and Artabazus defeat Tithraustes, 356.
—— conquers Sestos, 353.
Charidemus supports Cotys, who seizes Sestus, and claims the Chersonese, 360.
—— executed, 333.
Charilaus, king of Sparta, 884.
Charondas, the lawgiver of Catana, 640.

Chersonese, the, handed over to Athens, 358.
Chians, the, compelled by Athens to dismantle their walls, 425.
—— the, recover the command of the sea, 411.
Chilon of Sparta, 596.
—— Ephor at Sparta, 556.
Chionides, the comic poet, began to exhibit, 487.
Chios revolts from Athens, 412.
—— and Lacedaemon, alliance between, 412.
—— blockaded by the Athenians, 411.
—— allies defeat Athens at, 358.
Cimon conquers Eion and Scyrus, 471.
—— marches to aid the Lacedaemonians, 464.
—— banishment of, 461.
—— recalled, 457.
—— peace of, 444.
Cinadon, conspiracy of, 399.
Cinaethon of Lacedaemon, 770.
Cirrhaean or first Sacred War breaks out, 595.
Clazomenae revolts from Athens, but is recovered, 412.
Cleisthenes of Sicyon, victor in the second Pythiad, 582.
Cleisthenes of Athens, constitution of, 509.
—— expelled from Athens, 508.
Cleitus, murder of, 328.
Cleombrotus is sent to Thebes, 379.
—— invades Boeotia for the first time, 378.
—— slain at Leuctra, 371.
Cleomenes, king of Sparta, attacks Argolis, 520.
—— and Demaratus, kings of Sparta, 510.
—— dies, 491.
Cleon sent to Pylus instead of Nicias, 425.
—— sails to Chalcidice and retakes Torone, 422.
—— tries to recover Amphipolis and is slain, 422.

Cnidos, Conon defeats Peisander at, 394.
Codrus slain in battle against Dorians, 1066.
—— sons of, lead out colonies into Asia Minor, 1044.
Conon is made commander of the Athenian fleet, 407.
—— defeated by Callicratidas at Mitylene, 406.
—— defeats Peisander at Cnidos, 394.
—— rebuilds the walls of Athens, 393.
—— is imprisoned by Tiribazus, 392.
—— is sent by the Athenians to Tiribazus to operate against the Lacedaemonians, 392.
—— death of, 389.
Corcyra colonised by Corinthians, 734.
—— Alcidas and Brasidas sail to, 427.
—— massacre of the oligarchs at, 425.
—— taken by Timotheus, 375.
Corinth taken by Dorians, 1074.
—— conference of the allies at, 412.
Corinthians, the, defeated by the Athenians under Myronides, 458.
Coroebus, victory of, in Olympic games, 776.
Coronea, battle of, 447.
—— Agesilaus is victorious at, 394.
Cotys is assassinated, 360.
Crannon, battle of, 322.
Crates, the comic poet, 449.
Cratinus, the comic poet, 449.
Crissa taken by the Amphictyons under Eurylochus, 590.
Critias, one of the Thirty, quarrels with Theramenes, 404.
—— is slain, 403.
Croesus succeeds Alyattes in Lydia, 560.
Cromnus, siege of, 365.
Croton founded by the Achaeans, 710.

Ctesias, the historian, 384.
Cunaxa, Cyrus killed at, 401.
Cyaxares succeeds Phraortes in Media, 634.
—— takes Nineveh, 606.
Cylon attempts to become tyrant at Athens, 620.
Cyme colonised, 1033.
Cynoscephalae, the Thebans defeat Alexander at, but Pelopidas is killed, 363.
Cynossema, Peloponnesians defeated at, 411.
Cyprus reconquered by the Persians, 498.
—— conquered by Pausanias, 476.
Cypselus expels the Bacchiadae from Corinth, 655.
Cyrene founded by Battus of Thera, 631.
Cyrus I. defeats Astyages, 559.
—— takes Sardis, 546.
Cyrus II. co-operates with Lysander, 407.
Cythera captured by the Athenians under Nicias, 424.
—— captured by Conon and Pharnabazus, 393.
Cyzicus founded by Miletus, 756.
—— recolonised by Megara, 675.
—— defeat of the Lacedaemonians at, 410.

D

Damascus captured by Alexander, 333.
Damophon, king of Pisa, 588.
Darius recovers Persia from Pseudo-Smerdis, 521.
—— expedition against Scythia, 515.
—— demands earth and water of the Greeks, 491.
—— makes fresh preparations against Greece, 491.
—— dies, 485.
Darius II. begins to reign in Persia, 425.
—— dies, 405.

Darius Codomannus succeeds in Persia, 336.
Dascylium, Greek cavalry repulsed at, by Pharnabazus, 396.
Deceleia in Attica, occupied by the Spartans, 413.
Deioces, king of Media, according to Herodotus, 709-656.
Delians removed to Adramyttium, 422.
Delium, defeat of the Athenians at, 424.
Delos, confederacy of, organised, 475.
—— purification of, 426.
—— second purification of, 422.
—— second confederacy of, 378.
Delphi, the temple at, burnt, 458.
—— attacked by the Phocians, 448, 355.
Demades, peace of, between Athens and Philip, 338.
Demaratus and Cleomenes, kings of Sparta, 510.
—— of Sparta is deposed, 491.
Democritus is born, 460.
Demosthenes attacks Leucas and then the Aetolians, 426.
—— sent to Sicily, fortifies Pylus, 425.
—— comes to Syracuse with a fleet, 413.
—— fails in an attack on Epipolae, 413.
—— and Nicias capitulate, 413.
Demosthenes, the orator, born, 382.
—— "Against Androtion," 355.
—— "Against Leptines," and "On the Symmories," 354.
—— "For the Megalopolitans," "Against Timocrates," and "Against Aristocrates," 352.
—— "For the Rhodians," and "First Philippic," 351.
—— "Against Midias," 350.
—— Olynthiac orations, 349.
—— "On the Peace," 346.
—— "Second Philippic," 344.
—— "De Chersoneso," and "Third Philippic," 341.

Demosthenes, the orator, crowned at the Dionysia, 339.
—— "On the Crown," 330.
—— is condemned and fined, he leaves Athens, 324.
—— is recalled, 323.
—— dies at Calaureia, 322.
Dercyllidas goes to Lampsacus, and is continued in the command for another year, 398.
—— besieges Atarneus, 397.
Derdas and the Lacedaemonians repulse the Olynthians, 382.
—— repulses the Olynthians, 381.
Diocles, constitution and laws of, 412.
Dion, exiled from Syracuse by Dionysius, returns to Syracuse, 357.
—— is assassinated at Syracuse by Calippus, 353.
Dionysius I. becomes tyrant of Syracuse, 406.
—— fortifies Ortygia, 405.
—— makes peace with the Carthaginians, 405.
—— attempt to depose, which he frustrates, 405.
—— besieged in Ortygia, 404.
—— is supported by Sparta, 403.
—— conquers Naxus, Catana, and Leontini, 401.
—— double marriage of, 397.
—— besieges Motye, 397.
—— makes an alliance with Sparta, 395.
—— re-establishes Messene, 394.
—— fails in his attempt on Rhegium, 392.
—— takes Tauromenium, 391.
—— makes peace with the Carthaginians, 391.
—— fails to take Rhegium, 390.
—— defeats and captures the Italiot Greeks, 389.
—— restores Alcetas to Epirus, 385.
—— renews the war with Carthage and is totally defeated, 383.
—— of Syracuse assists the Spartans, 369.

Dionysius I. again assists the Spartans, 368.
—— gains the prize for Tragedy at the Lernaean festival, but dies soon after, 368.
Dionysius II. succeeds his father, 368.
—— returns to Syracuse, 345.
—— retires to Corinth, 344.
Diopithes in the Hellespont, 342.
Dorians invade the Peloponnese, 1103.
—— take Corinth, Sicyon, Troezen, Epidaurus, and Aegina, 1074.
—— colonise Melos, Cnidus, Halicarnassus, Rhodes, and part of Crete, 1066.
—— take Megara, 1066.
Dorieus of Lacedaemon, 510.
Draco's Laws, 621.

E

Ecdicus defeats Philocrates, the Athenian, 390.
Eetionea destroyed, 411.
Egesta and Selinus, quarrel between, 416, 409.
Egypt conquered by Cambyses, 525.
—— revolts from Persia, 486.
—— recovered by the Persians, 484.
Eira, capture of, 668.
Eleans defeat the Pisatans under Pyrrhus, 572.
—— seize Lasion, but the Arcadians defeat them, 366.
Eleusis, the Thirty are deposed and retire to, 403.
—— attack on, the generals are slain, 403.
Elis invaded by Agis, 401.
—— invaded by Agis, the second time, 400.
Empedocles floruit, 443.
Epaminondas at Leuctra, 371.
—— invades Peloponnesus, 369, 368, 867.
—— in Thessaly, 366.
—— in the Hellespont, 363.

Epaminondas invades Peloponnesus and falls at Mantinea, 362.
Ephesus, Tissaphernes defeats Thrasylus at, 410.
Epicharmus, the comedian, still exhibits in Syracuse, 485.
Epicydidas is sent to recall Agesilaus, 394.
Epidamnus founded by Corinth, 625 (cf. 435).
Epidaurus taken by Dorians, 1074.
—— and Argos at war, 419.
Epimenides of Crete visits Athens, 596.
Epipolae captured by the Athenians, 414.
Eretria liberated by the Athenians, 340.
Erinna of Lesbos, 610.
Erythrae revolts from Athens, 412.
Esarhaddon, king of Assyria, 681-667.
Eteonicus' soldiers conspire to seize the goods of the Chians and are detected, 406.
—— abandons Mitylene, 406.
Etna, eruption of, 425.
Euboea and Megara revolt from Athens, 445.
—— reconquered by Pericles, 445.
—— revolt of, 411.
—— revolts from the Thebans, 358.
Eucleides the philosopher, 399.
Eugammon of Cyrene, 566.
Eumelus, 761.
Euphron establishes himself at Sicyon, 367.
—— is assassinated in Thebes, 367.
Eupolis, the comic poet, exhibits "Maricas" and "Flatterers," 421.
Euripides, the tragic poet, 450.
—— the "Alcestis" of, 438.
—— the "Medea" of, 431.
—— the "Hippolytus" of, 428.
—— the "Suppliants" of, 420.
Eurylochus takes Crissa, 590.
—— marches to aid the Aetolians, 426.

Eurymedon, double victory of Cimon over the Persians at, 466.
Evagoras rescues Cyprus from the Phoenicians, 410.
—— conquers Tyre and Cilicia, 388.
—— is assassinated, 380.
Evarchus restored to Astacus by Corinth, 431.

G

Gaza, siege of, 332.
Gela founded by Rhodes and Crete, 690.
—— Sicilian states confer at, 424.
—— and Camarina taken by Imilcon, 405.
Gelo becomes tyrant of Gela, 491.
—— master of Syracuse, 485.
Gorgias, the Sophist, 419.
Granicus, battle of the, defeat of the Persians, 334.
Greeks, the, assemble at the Isthmus, 481.
Gyges, king of Lydia, (according to Herodotus), 716.
Gylippus, the Spartan, sent to Syracuse, 414.
—— defeats the Athenians, 414, 413.
Gylis, the polemarch, is slain while invading Locris, 394.

H.

Halicarnassus taken by Alexander, 334.
Halieis, Athens defeats Corinth and her allies at, 458.
Hannibal of Carthage invades Sicily, 409.
Harpalus, the satrap of Babylon, absconds to Greece with a large treasure, 324.
Hecataeus of Miletus, 500.
Hegemon's "Gigantomachia," 413.
Helots revolt from Sparta, the, 464.
Hephaestion, death of, 324.
Heraclea founded by the Spartans, 426.

Heraclea taken possession of by the Boeotians, 419.
—— destruction of the colonists, at, 409.
Heracleans defeated by the neighbouring tribes, 420.
Heraclea in Pontus founded by Miletus, 559.
Heracleitus of Ephesus, 504.
Here's temple at Argos burnt, 423.
Hermae, the affairs of the, 415.
Hermippus, the comic poet, 430.
Hermocrates of Syracuse, 424, 415.
—— brings Spartan reinforcements to Miletus, 412.
—— and the Syracusan generals deposed, 410.
—— attempts to force his way into Syracuse, 409.
—— again tries to enter Syracuse, but is slain, 408.
Herodas causes great alarm in Sparta by announcing that a large fleet is being prepared in Phoenicia, 396.
Herodotus born (about) 484.
Hesiod, poetry of, 884.
Hipparchus murdered, 514.
Hippias succeeds Peisistratus, 527.
—— expelled by Cleomenes and the Spartans, 510.
—— repairs to Sardis, 507.
—— at Marathon, 490.
Hippias of Elis, Sophist, 419.
Hippocrates, tyrant of Gela, 493.
Hippodamus, of Miletus, the architect, 443.
"*Hippolytus*," the, of Euripides, 428.
Hipponax of Ephesus, 532.
Hiero succeeds Gelo in Syracuse, 478.
—— tyrant of Syracuse and Gela, 476.
—— tyrant of Syracuse, dies, 467.
Himera founded by Zancle, 648.
—— defeat of Carthaginians by Thero and Gela at, 480.
Histiaeus allowed to return from Susa, 496.

Histiaeus retires to the Hellespont, 495.
—— at Chios; captured and put to death by Artaphernes, 494.
Homeric poems, possible date of, 950.
Hophrah succeeds Psammetichus II. in Egypt, 589.
Hyblaean Megara founded by Megara, 728.
Hyperbolus banished, 417.
Hyperides attacks Philocrates for his conduct in regard to Macedon, 343.
—— demanded by Alexander, 335.
—— death, 322.
Hyphasis, Alexander extends his conquest as far as the, 326.
Hysiae, defeat of Spartans by Argives at, 669.

I

Ibycus of Rhegium, 543.
Idomene, defeat of Spartans and Ambraciots at, 426.
Imilcon takes Gela and Camarina, 405.
—— starves himself to death, 395.
Inarus, the Athenians send an expedition to support, who had revolted from Persia, 460.
Ion of Chios, 450.
Ionians revolt from Persia, 499.
—— defeated at Ephesus, 499.
—— defeated at Lade, 494.
—— revolt entirely suppressed, 493.
Iphicrates destroys a Spartan mora, 392.
—— captures Sidus, Crommyon, and Oenoe, 392.
—— defeats the Phliasians, 393.
—— defeats and slays Anaxibius, 389.
—— takes nine out of ten ships sent by Dionysius to assist the Spartans, 372.
—— is sent to prevent the return of the Thebans, which he fails to do, 369.

Iphicrates retires from Thrace to Lesbos, 360.
—— in the Hellespont, 357.
Isaeus, the orator, 382.
Isagoras, archon of Athens, 508.
Ismenias is imprisoned and afterwards put to death, 383.
Isocrates, the orator, 382.
—— death of, 338.
Issus, defeat of Darius by Alexander at, 333.
Istros founded by Miletus, 654.

J

Jason of Pherae, rise of the power of, 375.
—— assassinated, 370.

L

Labotas, king of Sparta, 996.
Lacedaemonians, the, fail in their attempt on Stratus, 429.
—— found Heraclea, 426.
—— make an alliance with Athens for 50 years, 421.
—— make an alliance with the Boeotians, 421.
—— excluded from the Olympic festival, 420.
—— aid the Epidaurians, 418.
—— declare war on Athens, 413.
—— aid the Phocians against the Locrians, 395.
—— send a polemarch and a mora to Thespiae, and rebuild Plataea, 378.
—— defeated at Orchomenus, 375. See *Sparta*, and *Spartans*.
Laches captures Myle, 426.
Laconia attacked by the Athenians, 414.
Lade, defeat of the Ionian fleet at, 494.
Lamachus, death of, 414.
Lamian War, the, 323.
Lampsacus founded by Miletus, 654.
—— captured by Lysander, 405.

Lampsacus revolts from Athens, but is regained, 411.
Lechaeum, victory of the Lacedaemonians over the Argives at, 393.
Leonidas and Leotychides, kings of Sparta, 491.
—— is slain at Thermoplyae, 480.
Leontini founded by Naxos, 730.
—— revolution at, 422.
Leosthenes banished, 469.
—— defeats Antipater, but is slain, 323.
Leotychides and Leonidas, kings of Sparta, 491.
Lesbos colonised, 1053.
—— revolts, 428.
Lesches of Lesbos, 657.
Leucas founded by Corinth, 625.
—— Asopus defeated and killed at, 428.
Leucon, prince of the Hellespont, 386.
Leuctra, defeat of the Spartans at, 371.
—— Cleombrotus killed at, 371.
Lilybaeum, the Carthaginians defeat Dionysius at, 368.
Lipara founded by Cnidus and Rhodes, 579.
Locri in Italy, founded by Locrians, 673.
Locrians and Athenians, treaty between, 422.
Locris invaded by the Phocians, 395.
Lucanians, the, severely defeat the Thurians, 390.
Lycomedes, creates ill-feeling against the Thebans in Arcadia, 369.
—— for the Arcadians, negotiates a peace with Athens, 366.
Lycurgus, earliest date for, 996.
—— later date for, 884.
Lydia at war with Media, 615.
—— at peace with Miletus, 612.
Lysander sent by the Spartans to replace Cratesippidas, 408.
—— is sent out as epistoleus, 405.

Lysander captures Lampsacus, 405.
— sails into the Peiraeus, and the walls of Athens are pulled down, 404.
— sends a garrison to Athens to support the Thirty, 404.
— supports the Thirty with money and ships, 403.
— at Syracuse, 403.
— and the thirty Spartans recalled, 395.
— attacks Haliartus and is slain, 395.
Lysias, the orator, 393.

M

Magon and the Carthaginians make peace with Dionysius I., 391.
Mantinea, battle of, 418.
— Epaminondas defeats the Spartans at, but is killed, 362.
Mantineans, the, rebuild their wall, 370.
Marathon, Miltiades defeats the Persians at, 490.
Mardonius leads the first expedition of the Persians against Greece, 492.
— is left in Greece with 300,000 men, 480.
Massilia founded by Phocaea, 600.
Mausolus of Caria establishes oligarchies in Chios, Cos, and Rhodes, 355.
— dies, 351.
"*Medea*," the, of Euripides, 431.
Medes, the, who had revolted, now submit to Darius, 409.
Media at war with Lydia, 615.
Median Empire, beginning of, 687.
Megabazus' campaign in Thrace, etc., 514.
Megalopolis founded, 370.
Megara taken by Dorians, 1066.
— and Perinthus, sea-fight between, 565.
— long walls of, built, 461.
— and Euboea revolt from Athens, 445.

Megara invaded by Pericles, 431.
— lasting oligarchy in, 424.
Melanchrus of Mitylene overthrown by Pittacus, 611.
Melos taken by the Athenians, 416.
Memnon, death of, during the siege of Mitylene, 333.
Mende comes over to Brasidas, 423.
— recovered by the Athenians, 423.
Messenian war, first, 743-724.
— second, 688-668.
— third, 464-455.
Messene, Syracusans defeated at, 425.
— taken by the Carthaginians, 395.
— established by Dionysius, 394.
Methone attacked by Athens, 431.
Methymna, taken by Callicratidas, 407.
Micythus resigns the rule of Rhegium and Zancle, 467.
Midas of Phrygia commits suicide, 693.
Milesians, period of greatest power of the, 750.
Miletus at peace with Lydia, 612.
— conquered, 494.
— and Samos at war about Priene, 440.
— applies to Athens for help against Samos, 440.
— revolts from Athens, 412.
— the Athenians are victorious at, 412.
— taken by Alexander, 334.
Miltiades archon at Athens, 524.
— tyrant of the Chersonese, 515.
— retires from the Chersonese, 493.
— defeats the Persians at Marathon, 490.
— attacks Paros, fails, is condemned, and dies, 489.
Miltocythes revolts from Cotys and asks aid from Athens, 361.
Mimnermus of Colophon, 630.
Minoa captured by Nicias, 427.
Mitylene, blockade of, 428.

Mitylene blockaded by Paches, 428.
—— capitulates, 427.
—— and Methymna in Lesbos revolt from Athens, but are recovered, 412.
—— Conon defeats Callicratidas at, 406.
—— besieged, 333.
Mnasippus besieges Corcyra, 373.
Motye besieged by Dionysius, 397.
—— is taken by Dionysius, but retaken by Imilco, 396.
Mycale, victory of the Greek fleet at, 479.
Mycenae destroyed by the Argives, 468.
Myle captured by Laches, 426.
Myron, the sculptor, 445.

N

Nabopolassar frees Babylon from Assyria, 625.
Naucratis founded by Miletus in Egypt, 630.
Naupactus taken by the Athenians, 458.
—— given by Athens to the Messenians, 455.
Naxos founded by Chalcis, 735.
—— is reduced by the Athenians, 466.
Necho succeeds Psammetichus I. in Egypt, 615,
Nemea, battle of, 394.
Nemean games founded, 573.
Nineveh taken by Cyaxares, 606.
Nisaea conquered by the Athenians, 424.
—— reconquered by the Megarians, 409.
Notium, Antiochus is defeated by Lysander off, 407.

O

Ochus succeeds Artaxerxes in Persia, 359.
—— reduces Egypt to submission, 340.

Odessus founded by Miletus, 592.
Oenophyta, the Boeotians defeated by the Athenians at, 456.
Olpae, defeat of Spartans and Ambraciots at, 426.
Olynthus at war with Sparta, 383.
—— defeats Teleutias and the Spartans, 381.
—— surrenders to Polybiades, 379.
—— at war with Philip, 349.
—— fall of, 348.
Onomarchus succeeds Philomelus, 354.
—— conquers Coronea, 352.
—— is utterly defeated on the coast of Magnesia by Philip, 352.
Orchomenus besieged by the Argives, 418.
—— the Lacedaemonians defeated at, 375.
—— massacres at, by the Thebans, 370.
—— destroyed by the Thebans, 363.
"*Oresteia,*" the, of Aeschylus acted, 458.
Oreus liberated by the Athenians, Chalcidians, and Megarians, 341.
Oropus betrayed to the Boeotians, 411.
—— seized by exiles from Eretria, 366.
Orsippus of Megara, 720.
Orthagoras becomes tyrant of Sicyon, 670.

P

Paches blockades Miletus by land, 428.
—— at Notium, 427.
Pactolus, engagement between the Greeks and Persians on the, 395.
Pammenes, the Theban, marches to support Artabazus, in revolt against the king, 353.
Panactum betrayed to the Boeotians, 422.
—— destroyed, 420.
Panathenaea founded at Athens, 566.

Pantaleon, king of the Pisatans, 672.
Panyasis, an epic poet, 489.
Parium founded by the Milesians, Erythraeans, and Parians, 708.
Parmenides of Elea, 504.
Parmenio and his son executed in Philotas, 330.
Parthenon, the, at Athens completed, 438.
Pausanias conquers Cyprus, 476.
Pausanias is condemned to death, and goes into exile at Tegea, 395.
Peiraeum, the Athenians blockade the Spartan fleet in, 412.
—— failure of Spartan attack on, 429.
Peiraeus completed, 477.
Peisander, the epic poet, 648.
Peisander of Samos proposes the return of Alcibiades to Samos, 411.
Peisistratus, tyrant of Athens for first time, 560.
Pelopidas assists in liberating Thebes, 379.
—— marches to protect Larissa against Alexander of Pherae, 368.
—— in Thessaly, he is imprisoned by Alexander, 366.
—— is sent against Alexander of Pherae, 364.
—— slain at Cynocephalae, 363.
Peloponnese invaded by Dorians, 1103.
—— invaded by the Thebans for the first time, 369.
—— invaded by the Thebans for the second time, 369.
—— invaded the third time by the Thebans, 366.
—— for the fourth time, 362.
Peloponnesian War, the, 431-404.
Peloponnesians march to establish Isagoras at Athens, 507.
—— defeated by Phormio, 429.
—— defeated by Athens a second time, 429.
—— pass from Tissaphernes to Pharnabazus, 411.

Perdiccas I., king of Macedonia, 700.
Perdiccas II. attacked by Sitalces and the Athenians, 429.
Perdiccas II. joins the Athenians, 423.
—— blockaded by the Athenians, 417.
Perdiccas III. slain in battle against the Illyrians, 359.
Periander succeeds Cypselus at Corinth, 625.
—— dies, 585.
Pericles sole ruler at Athens, 444.
—— invades Megara, 431.
—— dies, 429.
Perinthus and Megara, sea-fight between, 565.
"*Persae*" of Aeschylus, 472.
Persia and Lacedaemon, first and second treaty between, 412.
—— and Sparta make a third treaty, 411.
—— in great disorder, 362.
Persian fleet almost entirely destroyed off Mount Athos, and the army in Thrace, 492.
—— war, first, 490.
—— war, second, 480.
—— fleet defeated at the Eurymedon, 466.
—— at Cyprus, 449.
—— fleet, the, takes Chios and Lesbos, 333.
Phalaris tyrant of Agrigentum, 572.
Pharnabazus invites a Spartan fleet to the Hellespont, 412.
—— supplies the Spartans with money and wood, 410.
—— retains the Athenian envoys for three years, and then sends them to the sea coast, 408.
—— repulses the Greek cavalry at Dascylium, 396.
—— invades Abydus, 394.
Phaselis in Lycia founded by Dorians, 690.
Phayllus falls while invading eastern Locris, 352.

Pheidias, the sculptor, 445.
—— at Olympia, 436.
—— death of, 431.
Pheidon, king of Argos, drives out the Eleans, 748.
Pherecydes of Syros, 560.
Philip II. succeeds in Macedon, 359.
—— withdraws from Amphipolis, and defeats the Paeonians and Illyrians, 359.
—— besieges Amphipolis, 358.
—— conquers Amphipolis, 357.
—— defeats the Illyrians, 356.
—— takes Abdera, Maronea, and Methone, 353.
—— defeats Phayllus, but is severely defeated by Onomarchus twice, 353.
—— takes Pherae and Pagasae, 352.
—— falls sick and retires from Thrace, 352.
—— attacks Arybbas, king of the Molossi, 351.
—— at war with Olynthus, 349.
—— celebrates Olympic games in Macedon, 348.
—— negotiations for peace between Athens and, 347.
—— chosen to preside over the Pythian games, 346.
—— attacks the Illyrians, Dardanians, and Triballi, 345.
—— makes an attempt on Megara which fails, 343.
—— establishes Philistides as tyrant in Oreus, 343.
—— establishes Alexander in Epirus in the room of Arybbas, 343.
—— establishes his power in Euboea, 343.
—— in Thrace, 341.
—— besieges Selymbria, Perinthus, and Byzantium, 340.
—— at the head of the Amphictyons defeats the Amphisseans, 339.
—— raises the siege of Byzantium and marches into Scythia, 339.

Philip II. marries Cleopatra, 337.
—— assassinated at his daughter's marriage, 336.
Philippi founded, 356.
Philistus, the historian, 397.
Philocrates, peace of, 346.
—— goes into exile, 343.
Philolaus gives laws to the Thebans, 728.
Philomelus and the Phocians are defeated by the Thebans, and himself slain, 354.
Philoxenus, the dithyrambic poet, 398.
Phliasian exiles, the, demand of the Lacedaemonians to be restored to Phlius, 383.
Phlius besieged by Agesilaus, 380.
Phocaeans, the, attain great power by sea, 575.
—— expelled from home by Harpagus, 543.
Phocian, the, or third Sacred War breaks out, 355.
Phocians, the, attack Delphi, 448.
—— the, invade Locris, 395.
—— destruction of the, 346.
Phocylides of Miletus, 532.
Phoebidas seizes the Cadmea with the assistance of Leontiades, 383.
—— ravages Boeotia, but is slain by the Theban cavalry, 378.
Phormio at Naupactus, 430.
—— defeats the Peloponnesians in the gulf of Corinth, 429.
Phraortes ascends the throne of Media, 656.
Phrynichus wrote the "Capture of Miletus," 491.
Phrynichus assassinated, 411.
Pindar, the lyric poet, 480.
Pisatans under Pyrrhus defeated by the Eleans, 572.
Pittacus overthrows Melanchrus, tyrant of Mitylene, 611.
—— is "aesymnete" of Miletus, 589.

Plataea seeks the protection of Athens, 519.
— defeat of Persians by the Hellenes at, 479.
— attacked by the Thebans, 431.
— besieged by the Peloponnesians, 429.
— surrenders, 427.
— destroyed by the Thebans, 374.
Plato, the philosopher, 399.
— visits Dionysius II. 368, 361.
Plato, the comic poet, 391.
Pleistarchus succeeds Leonidas as king, 480.
Pleistoanax of Sparta invades Attica, 445.
Plutarch of Eretria applies to Athens for help, 351.
Polycleitus, the sculptor, 445.
Polycrates, tyrant of Samos, 532.
— attacked by the Lacedaemonians, 525.
— killed by Oroetes, 522.
Polydorus succeeds Jason, 370.
— is slain by Polyphron, his brother, 370.
Polygnotus, the painter, 445.
Polyphron is slain by Alexander of Pherae, 370.
Porus is defeated by Alexander, 326.
Potidaea revolts from Athens, 432.
— capitulates, 430.
Procles, tyrant of Epidaurus, 625.
Prodicus, the Sophist, 419.
Propylaea, the, completed at Athens, 433.
Protagoras (born 482, died 411), 421.
Psammenitus succeeds Amasis in Egypt, 526.
Psammetichus, last tyrant of Corinth, 585.
Psammetichus I., king of Egypt, 650.
Psammetichus II., king of Egypt, 595.
Pseudo-Smerdis usurps in Persia for seven months, 521.
Pygela, Thrasylus defeats the Milesians at, 410.
Pylus blockaded by the Spartans, 425.
— the Lacedaemonians surrender at, 425.
— attempt to recover, 425.
— is retained by Athens, 421.
— reconquered by the Spartans, 409.
Pythagoras of Samos victorious in boxing at Olympia, 588.
Pythian games reinstituted or extended, 586.

R

Rhegium founded by Chalcis, 743.
Rhodes revolts from Athens, 411.
Rhoeteum and Antandros taken by Lesbian refugees, 424.
— battle at, 411.

S

Sacadas of Argos gains the prize for the flutes in the first three Pythiads, 585.
Sadyattes, king of Lydia, 629-617.
— of Lydia at war with Miletus, 623.
Salamis in Cyprus, victory of Athenians over the Persians at, 449.
Salamis, the Greeks defeat Xerxes at, 480.
Samian exiles at Zancle in Sicily, 494.
Samius, the Spartan admiral, cooperates with Cyrus against Artaxerxes, 402.
Samos, revolution at, 565,
— and Miletus at war about Priene, 440.
— besieged for nine months, 440.
— conquered, 439.
— revolution at, 412.
— capitulates to Lysander, 404.
Sappho of Lesbos, 610.
Sardis taken by the Cimmerians, 635.

Sardis taken by Cyrus, 546.
—— burnt by the Ionians, 499.
Sargon, king of Assyria, 721-704.
Scione captured by Brasidas, 423.
—— retaken by the Athenians, 421.
Selinus founded by Hyblaean Megara, 628.
—— and Egesta, quarrel between, 416 (cf. 409).
Selymbria founded by Megara, 660.
Sennacherib, king of Assyria, 704-681.
Shalmanesar V., king of Assyria, 726-721.
Sicilian expedition of Athens, 415.
Sicily, invasion of, by the Carthaginians, 409, 406 (cf. 383, 368).
Sicyon taken by Dorians, 1074.
Simonides, the lyric poet, 480.
Sinope founded by Miletus, 770.
Sitalces forms an alliance with Athens, 431.
Smyrna colonised, 1015.
Socrates, 419.
—— death of, 399.
Solon, archon at Athens, 594.
Solygea, the Athenians attack the Corinthians at, 425.
Sophocles is born, 495.
—— obtains a victory over Aeschylus, 468.
—— death of, 406.
Sparta, earthquake at, 464.
—— congress at, 432.
—— enters into alliance with Dionysius I., 395.
Spartans conquer Messenia, 724, 668.
—— overthrow the tyranny in Corinth, 581.
—— compel the Mantineans to pull down their walls, 385.
—— march against the Illyrians, 384.
—— at war with Olynthus, 383.
—— aid the Tegeate exiles, 370.
—— take Carya, invade the Parrhasia, and defeat the Arcadians, 368.

Sphacteria, Spartans cut off in, 425. (See *Pylus*.)
Sphodrias attempts to seize Peiraeus, 378.
Stagira in Chalcidice, founded by Andros, 654.
"*Stesichorus*" of Himera, 610.
Strattis, the comedian, 393.
Strouthas defeats Thimbron, 391.
Sunium fortified by the Athenians, 413.
Susa, embassy of the Greeks to, 367.
Sybaris founded by Achaeans, 721.
—— destroyed by Croton, 510.
Sybarites defeated by the Crotoniates, 447.
Sybota, naval engagement at, 432.
Syracuse founded by Archias of Corinth, 734.
—— establishment of democracy at, 466.
—— at war with Leontini, 427.
—— extreme form of democracy in, 412.
—— prepares a fleet, 398.
Syracusan army in mutiny, 404.

T

Tamynae, battle of, 350.
Tanagra, the Athenians defeated by the Spartans at, 457.
Tarentum founded by the Parthenii from Sparta, 708.
Tauromenium, Dionysius repulsed at, 394.
—— taken by Dionysius, 391.
Tegea acknowledges the hegemony of Sparta, 554.
—— attacked by the Argives, 418.
Telestes, the dithyrambic poet, 398.
Teleutias, with the Aeginetans, attacks the Peiraeus and carries off much booty, 389.
—— is sent to Olynthus with troops, 382.
—— and the Lacedaemonians entirely defeated by the Olynthians, 381.
—— death of, 381.

Thaletas the Cretan, 665.
Thasos colonised by the Parians, 708.
—— reduced by Athens, 463.
—— revolt of, 410.
Theagenes, tyrant of Megara, 625.
Thebans, the, attack Plataea, 431.
—— victorious at Leuctra, 371.
—— wish to destroy the remnant of the Lacedaemonians, but are dissuaded from their purpose by Jason, 371.
—— destroy Plataea, 374.
—— invade Peloponnesus, restore Messenia, and rebuild Messene, 369.
—— invade Thessaly and deliver Pelopidas, 365.
—— victorious at Mantinea, 362.
—— ask Philip's aid against the Phocians, 347.
—— capitulation of the, 338.
Thebes dismantles Thespiae, 423.
—— the liberation of, 379.
—— state congress at, 366.
—— sends out a fleet to the Hellespont under Epaminondas, 363.
—— revolt of, 335.
Themistocles, archon at Athens, 493.
—— archon of Athens, 482.
—— ostracised, 471.
Theognis of Megara, 543.
Theopompus, king of Sparta, 743.
Thespis of Icaria, 535.
Thera colonised, 1074.
Theramenes attacks the generals in the assembly, 406.
—— is sent to Lysander to ask for peace, 405.
—— sent to Sparta with nine others with full powers to make peace, 404.
—— put to death at the instance of Critias, 404.
Thero, tyrant of Agrigentum, 489.
—— dies, 472.
Thessalians invade Thessaly, 1133.
Thimbron is sent out as harmost, 400.

Thimbron is joined by the remnant of the Ten Thousand, 399.
—— is defeated and killed by Strouthas, 391.
Thrasybulus tyrant of Miletus, 612.
Thrasybulus succeeds Hiero in Syracuse, 467.
Thrasybulus repulses a sortie from Deceleia, 410.
—— reduces towns in Thrace and Thasos, 408.
—— with 70 followers, goes to Phyle, 403.
—— defeats the Lacedaemonian garrison sent to besiege Phyle, 403.
—— is slain at Aspendus, 390.
Thrasydaeus, defeated by Hiero, 472.
Thrasylus returns to Athens, 408.
Thurians, the, severely defeated by the Lucanians, 390.
Thurii founded by the Athenians, 443.
Thucydides banished, 424.
—— history ends, 411.
Thyrea captured by the Athenians, 424.
Tiglath-Pilesar II., king of Assyria, 745-726.
Timocreon of Rhodes, lyric poet, 471.
Timoleon leaves Corinth for Syracuse, 344.
—— defeats the Carthaginians in Sicily on the Crimesus, 340.
—— dies at Syracuse, 337.
Timotheus, the dithyrambic poet, 398.
—— takes Corcyra, and defeats the Spartans under Nicolochus at Alyzia, 375.
—— is sent to aid Corcyra, but is superseded by Iphicrates and Chabrias, 372.
—— is sent with a fleet to assist Ariobarzanus, and takes Samos, 366.
—— acts against Cotys, king of Thrace, and supersedes Iphicrates, 365.

Timotheus fails to recover Amphipolis, 365.
—— superseded by Ergophilus, 362.
—— attacks the allies and is defeated, 357.
—— dies at Chalcis, 354.
Tissaphernes assists the Chians and Erythraeans against Athens, 412.
—— makes an alliance with Sparta, 412.
—— quarrels with the Peloponnesians, 411.
—— takes Alcibiades prisoner to Sardis, 411.
—— arrives at Ephesus, 411.
—— is made satrap of Sardis, 400.
—— declares war on Agesilaus, 396.
—— put to death by Tithraustes, who succeeds him, 395.
Tithraustes sends Timocrates to stir up the Greek states against Sparta, 395.
Torone taken by Brasidas, 424.
—— recaptured by Cleon, 422.
Tralles and Magnesia submit to Alexander, Parmenio is sent to take possession of them, 334.

Trapezus founded by Sinope, 757.
—— the Ten Thousand return to, 401.
Troezen taken by Dorians, 1074.
Troy, fall of. 1183 B.C. (see note.)
Tuscans defeated by Hiero, 474.
Tyre, siege of, 332.
Tyrtaeus came from Athens to Sparta about 683.

X

Xanthippus archon at Athens, 479.
Xanthus, the Lydian, an historian, 463.
Xenarchus, the son of Sophron, the author of "Mimes," 392.
Xenophanes "floruit," 540.
Xenophon, the historian, 397.
Xerxes becomes king of Persia, 485.
—— winters at Sardis, 481.
—— defeated by the Greeks at Salamis, 480.
—— assassinated by Artabanus, 465.

Z

Zaleucus gives laws to the Locrians, 660.
Zeno, the philosopher, 448.

Crown 8vo. 4s. 6d.
ELEMENTS OF GREEK ACCIDENCE. By EVELYN ABBOTT, M.A., LL.D., Fellow and Tutor of Balliol College, Oxford.

Small 8vo. 3s. 6d.
SELECTIONS FROM LUCIAN. With English Notes. By EVELYN ABBOTT, M.A., LL.D.

New Edition, Revised. Crown 8vo. 3s. 6d.
ARNOLD'S PRACTICAL INTRODUCTION TO GREEK PROSE COMPOSITION. By EVELYN ABBOTT, M.A., LL.D.

8vo. 16s.
HELLENICA. A Collection of Essays on Greek Poetry, Philosophy, History, and Religion. Edited by EVELYN ABBOTT, M.A., LL.D.

Crown 8vo. 3s. 6d.
A PRIMER OF GREEK GRAMMAR. With a Preface by JOHN PERCIVAL, M.A., LL.D., President of Trinity College, Oxford; late Head Master of Clifton College.

Or separately, Crown 8vo. 2s. 6d.
ACCIDENCE. By EVELYN ABBOTT, M.A., LL.D., Fellow and Tutor of Balliol College, Oxford; and E. D. MANSFIELD, M.A., Assistant Master at Clifton College.

Crown 8vo. 1s. 6d.
SYNTAX. By E. D. MANSFIELD, M.A., Assistant Master at Clifton College.

www.ingramcontent.com/pod-product-compliance
Lightning Source LLC
Chambersburg PA
CBHW030818190426
43197CB00036B/591